HMH SCIENCE DIMENSIONS™
ENGINEERING AND SCIENCE

Module A

This Write-In Book belongs to

_____

Teacher/Room

_____

Houghton Mifflin Harcourt™

Consulting Authors

Michael A. DiSpezio

Global Educator
North Falmouth, Massachusetts

Michael DiSpezio has authored many HMH instructional programs for Science and Mathematics. He has also authored numerous trade books and multimedia programs on various topics and hosted dozens of studio and location broadcasts for various organizations in the U.S. and worldwide. Most recently, he has been working with educators to provide strategies for implementing the Next Generation Science Standards, particularly the science and engineering practices, cross-cutting concepts, and the use of Evidence Notebooks. To all his projects, he brings his extensive background in science, his expertise in classroom teaching at the elementary, middle, and high school levels, and his deep experience in producing interactive and engaging instructional materials.

Marjorie Frank

Science Writer and Content-Area Reading Specialist
Brooklyn, New York

An educator and linguist by training, a writer and poet by nature, Marjorie Frank has authored and designed a generation of instructional materials in all subject areas, including past HMH Science programs. Her other credits include authoring science issues of an award-winning children's magazine, writing game-based digital assessments, developing blended learning materials for young children, and serving as instructional designer and co-author of pioneering school-to-work software. In addition, she has served on the adjunct faculty of Hunter, Manhattan, and Brooklyn Colleges, teaching courses in science methods, literacy, and writing. For *HMH Science Dimensions™*, she has guided the development of our K–2 strands and our approach to making connections between NGSS and Common Core ELA/literacy standards.

Acknowledgments

Cover credits: (toothpick bridge) ©Houghton Mifflin Harcourt; (watermelon) ©malerapaso/Getty Images; (modern bridge) ©dvoevnore/Shutterstock.

Section Header Master Art: (machinations) ©DNY59/E+/Getty Images

Printed in the U.S.A.

ISBN   978-0-544-86106-0

4 5 6 7 8 9 10 0877 25 24 23 22 21 20 19 18 17

4500645471   A B C D E F G

Michael R. Heithaus, Ph.D.

Dean, College Of Arts, Sciences & Education
Professor, Department Of Biological Sciences
Florida International University
Miami, Florida

Mike Heithaus joined the FIU Biology Department in 2003, has served as Director of the Marine Sciences Program and Executive Director of the School of Environment, Arts, and Society, which brings together the natural and social sciences and humanities to develop solutions to today's environmental challenges. He now serves as Dean of the College of Arts, Sciences & Education. His research focuses on predator-prey interactions and the ecological importance of large marine species. He has helped to guide the development of Life Science content in *HMH Science Dimensions™*, with a focus on strategies for teaching challenging content as well as the science and engineering practices of analyzing data and using computational thinking.

Cary I. Sneider, Ph.D.

Associate Research Professor
Portland State University
Portland, Oregon

While studying astrophysics at Harvard, Cary Sneider volunteered to teach in an Upward Bound program and discovered his real calling as a science teacher. After teaching middle and high school science in Maine, California, Costa Rica and Micronesia, he settled for nearly three decades at Lawrence Hall of Science in Berkeley, California, where he developed skills in curriculum development and teacher education. Over his career Cary directed more than 20 federal, state, and foundation grant projects, and was a writing team leader for the Next Generation Science Standards. He has been instrumental in ensuring *HMH Science Dimensions™* meets the high expectations of the NGSS and provides an effective three-dimensional learning experience for all students.

Program Advisors

Paul D. Asimow
Eleanor and John R. McMillan Professor of Geology and Geochemistry
California Institute of Technology
Pasadena, California

Dr. Eileen Cashman
Professor
Humboldt State University
Arcata, California

Elizabeth A. De Stasio
Raymond J. Herzog Professor of Science
Lawrence University
Appleton, Wisconsin

Perry Donham
Lecturer
Boston University
Boston, Massachusetts

Shila Garg, Ph.D.
Emerita Professor of Physics
Former Dean of Faculty & Provost
The College of Wooster
Wooster, Ohio

Tatiana A. Krivosheev
Professor of Physics
Clayton State University
Morrow, Georgia

Mark B. Moldwin
Professor of Space Sciences and Engineering
University of Michigan
Ann Arbor, Michigan

Kelly Y. Neiles, Ph.D.
Assistant Professor of Chemistry
St. Mary's College of Maryland
St. Mary's City, Maryland

Dr. Sten Odenwald
Astronomer
NASA Goddard Spaceflight Center
Greenbelt, Maryland

Bruce W. Schafer
Executive Director
Oregon Robotics Tournament & Outreach Program
Beaverton, Oregon

Barry A. Van Deman
President and CEO
Museum of Life and Science
Durham, North Carolina

Kim Withers, Ph.D.
Assistant Professor
Texas A&M University-Corpus Christi
Corpus Christi, Texas

Adam D. Woods, Ph.D.
Professor
California State University, Fullerton
Fullerton, California

Classroom Reviewers

Cynthia Book, Ph.D.
John Barrett Middle School
Carmichael, California

Katherine Carter, M.Ed.
Fremont Unified School District
Fremont, California

Theresa Hollenbeck, M.Ed.
Winston Churchill Middle School
Carmichael, California

Kathryn S. King
Science and AVID Teacher
Norwood Jr. High School
Sacramento, California

Donna Lee
Science/STEM Teacher
Junction Ave. K8
Livermore, California

Rebecca S. Lewis
Science Teacher
North Rockford Middle School
Rockford, Michigan

Bryce McCourt
8th Grade Science Teacher/Middle School Curriculum Chair
Cudahy Middle School
Cudahy, Wisconsin

Sarah Mrozinski
Teacher
St. Sebastian School
Milwaukee, Wisconsin

Raymond Pietersen
Science Program Specialist
Elk Grove Unified School District
Elk Grove, California

Richard M. Stec, M.A.– Curriculum, Instruction, and Supervision
District Science Supervisor
West Windsor-Plainsboro
Regional School District
West Windsor, New Jersey

Anne Vitale
STEM Supervisor
Randolph Middle School
Randolph, New Jersey

© Houghton Mifflin Harcourt

You are a scientist!
You are naturally curious.

Have you ever wondered . . .

- why is it difficult to catch a fly?
- how a new island can appear in an ocean?
- how to design a great tree house?
- how a spacecraft can send messages across the solar system?

HMH SCIENCE DIMENSIONS™

will *SPARK* your curiosity!

AND prepare you for

✓	tomorrow
✓	next year
✓	college or career
✓	life!

Where do you see yourself in 15 years?

Observe

Collect
Data

Be a scientist.
Work like real scientists work.

Analyze

Be an engineer.
Solve problems like engineers do.

Define Problems

Test Solutions

STEM

Gather Information

Think Critically

Explain your world.
Start by asking questions.

Conduct Investigations

Collaborate

Develop Explanations

Construct Arguments

There's more than one way to the answer. What's YOURS?

YOUR Program

Write-In Book:

• a brand-new and innovative textbook that will guide you through your next generation curriculum, including your hands-on lab program

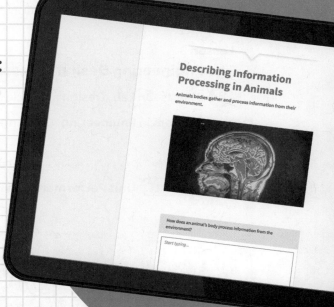

Interactive Online Student Edition:

• a complete online version of your textbook enriched with videos, interactivities, animations, simulations, and room to enter data, draw, and store your work

More tools are available online to help you practice and learn science, including:

• **Hands-On Labs**

• **Science and Engineering Practices Handbook**

• **Crosscutting Concepts Handbook**

• **English Language Arts Handbook**

• **Math Handbook**

Contents

Roller coaster design needs to meet the need for both a fun and a safe amusement park experience.

© Houghton Mifflin Harcourt • Image Credits: ©China-FotoPre ss via Getty Images/Getty Images

Contents

UNIT 2

The Practices of Engineering

The challenge for participants in gravity racing is to build the fastest car possible using no engine.

Whether you are in the lab or in the field, you are responsible for your own safety and the safety of others. To fulfill these responsibilities and avoid accidents, be aware of the safety of your classmates as well as your own safety at all times. Take your lab work and field work seriously, and behave appropriately. Elements of safety to keep in mind are shown below and on the following pages.

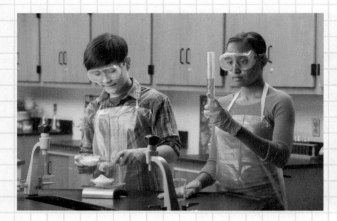 

Safety in the Lab

☐ Be sure you understand the materials, your procedure, and the safety rules before you start an investigation in the lab.

☐ Know where to find and how to use fire extinguishers, eyewash stations, shower stations, and emergency power shut-offs.

☐ Use proper safety equipment. Always wear personal protective equipment, such as eye protection and gloves, when setting up labs, during labs, and when cleaning up.

☐ Do not begin until your teacher has told you to start. Follow directions.

☐ Keep the lab neat and uncluttered. Clean up when you are finished. Report all spills to your teacher immediately. Watch for slip/fall and trip/fall hazards.

☐ If you or another student are injured in any way, tell your teacher immediately, even if the injury seems minor.

☐ Do not take any food or drink into the lab. Never take any chemicals out of the lab.

Safety in the Field

☐ Be sure you understand the goal of your fieldwork and the proper way to carry out the investigation before you begin fieldwork.

☐ Use proper safety equipment and personal protective equipment, such as eye protection, that suits the terrain and the weather.

☐ Follow directions, including appropriate safety procedures as provided by your teacher.

☐ Do not approach or touch wild animals. Do not touch plants unless instructed by your teacher to do so. Leave natural areas as you found them.

☐ Stay with your group.

☐ Use proper accident procedures, and let your teacher know about a hazard in the environment or an accident immediately, even if the hazard or accident seems minor.

Safety Symbols

To highlight specific types of precautions, the following symbols are used throughout the lab program. Remember that no matter what safety symbols you see within each lab, all safety rules should be followed at all times.

Dress Code

- Wear safety goggles (or safety glasses as appropriate for the activity) at all times in the lab as directed. If chemicals get into your eye, flush your eyes immediately for a minimum of 15 minutes.
- Do not wear contact lenses in the lab.
- Do not look directly at the sun or any intense light source or laser.
- Wear appropriate protective non-latex gloves as directed.
- Wear an apron or lab coat at all times in the lab as directed.
- Tie back long hair, secure loose clothing, and remove loose jewelry. Remove acrylic nails when working with active flames.
- Do not wear open-toed shoes, sandals, or canvas shoes in the lab.

Glassware and Sharp Object Safety

- Do not use chipped or cracked glassware.
- Use heat-resistant glassware for heating or storing hot materials.
- Notify your teacher immediately if a piece of glass breaks.
- Use extreme care when handling any sharp and pointed instruments.
- Do not cut an object while holding the object unsupported in your hands. Place the object on a suitable cutting surface, and always cut in a direction away from your body.

Chemical Safety

- If a chemical gets on your skin, on your clothing, or in your eyes, rinse it immediately for a minimum of 15 minutes (using the shower, faucet, or eyewash station), and alert your teacher.
- Do not clean up spilled chemicals unless your teacher directs you to do so.
- Do not inhale any gas or vapor unless directed to do so by your teacher. If you are instructed to note the odor of a substance, wave the fumes toward your nose with your hand. This is called wafting. Never put your nose close to the source of the odor.
- Handle materials that emit vapors or gases in a well-ventilated area.
- Keep your hands away from your face while you are working on any activity.

Safety Symbols, continued

Electrical Safety

- Do not use equipment with frayed electrical cords or loose plugs.
- Do not use electrical equipment near water or when clothing or hands are wet.
- Hold the plug housing when you plug in or unplug equipment. Do not pull on the cord.
- Use only GFI protected electrical receptacles.

Heating and Fire Safety

- Be aware of any source of flames, sparks, or heat (such as flames, heating coils, or hot plates) before working with any flammable substances.
- Know the location of lab fire extinguisher and fire-safety blankets.
- Know your school's fire-evacuation routes.
- If your clothing catches on fire, walk to the lab shower to put out the fire. Do not run.
- Never leave a hot plate unattended while it is turned on or while it is cooling.
- Use tongs or appropriate insulated holders when handling heated objects.
- Allow all equipment to cool before storing it.

Plant and Animal Safety

- Do not eat any part of a plant.
- Do not pick any wild plant unless your teacher instructs you to do so.
- Handle animals only as your teacher directs.
- Treat animals carefully and respectfully.
- Wash your hands throughly with soap and water after handling any plant or animal.

Cleanup

- Clean all work surfaces and protective equipment as directed by your teacher.
- Dispose of hazardous materials or sharp objects only as directed by your teacher.
- Wash your hands throughly with soap and water before you leave the lab or after any activity.

Name: _____   Date: _____

Student Safety Quiz

Circle the letter of the BEST answer.

1. Before starting an investigation or lab procedure, you should
   A. try an experiment of your own
   B. open all containers and packages
   C. read all directions and make sure you understand them
   D. handle all the equipment to become familiar with it

2. At the end of any activity you should
   A. wash your hands thoroughly with soap and water before leaving the lab
   B. cover your face with your hands
   C. put on your safety goggles
   D. leave hot plates switched on

3. If you get hurt or injured in any way, you should
   A. tell your teacher immediately
   B. find bandages or a first aid kit
   C. go to your principal's office
   D. get help after you finish the lab

4. If your glassware is chipped or broken, you should
   A. use it only for solid materials
   B. give it to your teacher for recycling or disposal
   C. put it back into the storage cabinet
   D. increase the damage so that it is obvious

5. If you have unused chemicals after finishing a procedure, you should
   A. pour them down a sink or drain
   B. mix them all together in a bucket
   C. put them back into their original containers
   D. dispose of them as directed by your teacher

6. If electrical equipment has a frayed cord, you should
   A. unplug the equipment by pulling the cord
   B. let the cord hang over the side of a counter or table
   C. tell your teacher about the problem immediately
   D. wrap tape around the cord to repair it

7. If you need to determine the odor of a chemical or a solution, you should
   A. use your hand to bring fumes from the container to your nose
   B. bring the container under your nose and inhale deeply
   C. tell your teacher immediately
   D. use odor-sensing equipment

8. When working with materials that might fly into the air and hurt someone's eye, you should wear
   A. goggles
   B. an apron
   C. gloves
   D. a hat

9. Before doing experiments involving a heat source, you should know the location of the
   A. door
   B. window
   C. fire extinguisher
   D. overhead lights

10. If you get chemicals in your eye you should
   A. wash your hands immediately
   B. put the lid back on the chemical container
   C. wait to see if your eye becomes irritated
   D. use the eyewash station right away, for a minimum of 15 minutes

Go online to view the Lab Safety Handbook for additional information.

UNIT 1

Introduction to Engineering and Science

The Falkirk Wheel is a rotating boat lift that connects two major waterways in Scotland. It is an example of how technology and science allow engineers to create tools to solve modern problems.

Throughout history, humans have used objects, tools, and processes to improve their lives. As scientific discoveries have progressed and technology has advanced, the connections between engineering, science, and society have become even greater. In this unit, you will explore these connections. You will also investigate how scientists and engineers use systems and system models as they work through the engineering design process.

Why It Matters

Here are some questions to consider as you work through the unit. Can you answer any of the questions now? Revisit these questions at the end of the unit to apply what you discover.

Questions	Notes
How have you observed technology solving problems in your everyday life?	
What changes in technology have you seen in your lifetime?	
What impacts have these changes had on you and your community?	
What problems in society could benefit from developments in technology?	
Which members of your community would benefit the most from solving these problems?	

Unit Starter: Asking Questions and Defining Problems

Think about how your arms would feel if you were holding a heavy bucket for a long time. Identify the most important issues necessary to define the problem and investigate solutions in the photo below.

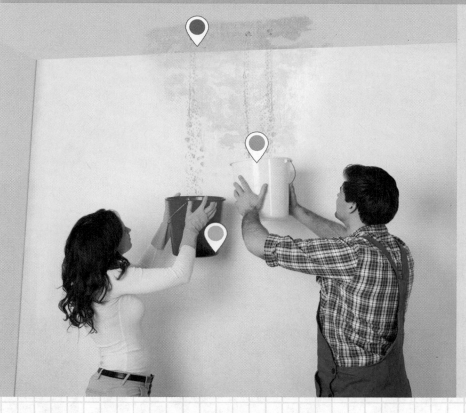

The ceiling is leaking, which is causing a problem for these homeowners.

The homeowners are using buckets to catch the water. The buckets are the first solution to this problem.

As more water collects in the buckets, they become heavier and more difficult to hold.

1. The original problem in the image is that the ceiling is leaking. Another problem is that the buckets are heavy and hard to hold. Select all the questions that the homeowners could ask about their next steps in solving the problem.

   A. Is there a better way to hold the buckets?

   B. Is the problem in the ceiling or the roof above?

   C. What is the ceiling made of?

   D. What paint color should we use to repaint?

 Go online to download the Unit Project Worksheet to help you plan your project.

Unit Project

Solution Power!

Can you make your community better with technology? Find a problem in your community that inspires you to find a better solution. Research and develop a proposal for how to best solve this problem.

Engineering, Science, and Society

A ferry system provided transport between the boroughs of New York long before bridges were built. The Staten Island Ferry service is one of the last remaining services.

© Houghton Mifflin Harcourt • Image Credits: ©Marceux/Photographer's Choice/Getty Images

By the end of this lesson . . .

you will be able to describe the relationships between engineering, science, and society.

CAN YOU EXPLAIN IT?

What needs influenced the development of mosquito netting?

Insecticide-treated mosquito nets help prevent the spread of malaria in developing countries. Malaria is spread by mosquito bites. The nets must meet the needs of the people who use them. The nets must be affordable, lightweight, easy to install, and be usable for a long time.

1. Which of the following factors often influences the design and development of engineering solutions? Circle all that apply.

   A. scientific findings

   B. availability of natural resources

   C. needs and wants of society

   D. needs and wants of individuals

   E. total cost of the solution

2. Does the best solution to an engineering problem have to address every need of its users? Explain your answer.

 EVIDENCE NOTEBOOK As you explore the lesson, gather evidence to help explain how various factors can influence the development of a technology.

Relating Science, Engineering, and Technology

Science is the study of the natural world. It is a search for knowledge about how nature works. Scientific discoveries improve or change our understanding of natural phenomena. Engineering is an area of study related to science. **Engineering** is the use and application of science and math to solve problems. The solutions designed and built by engineers are examples of technology. **Technology** is any tool, process, or system that is designed to solve a problem. The designed world includes all parts of the environment that were made by people. You are surrounded by the designed world. You depend on it. The designed world exists within the natural world.

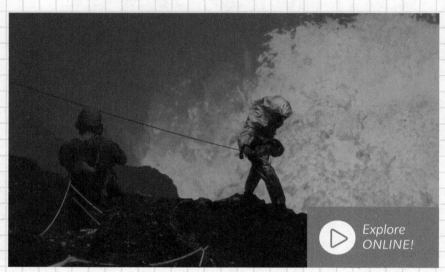

A volcanologist walks near the vent of an active volcano. Lava can range in temperature from 700°C–1250°C (approximately 1200°F–2200°F).

Explore ONLINE!

3. **Discuss** Together with a partner, review the photo above. This scientist depends on several engineered items to carry out his or her research. What might the purpose of some of those items be?

Scientists Use Engineered Tools to Explore the Natural World

Scientific discoveries help increase our understanding of the world around us. Scientists often rely on engineered tools, such as computers and measuring devices, to carry out research. These tools "extend" our senses and abilities. They allow us to sense and process events that would otherwise be invisible to us. For example, telescopes allow us to see phenomena that are too far away for human eyes to see. Computers quickly carry out calculations that would take a human brain much longer to do.

Many of Earth's natural phenomena are difficult to observe directly. Engineers may design materials and systems to aid scientific study. For example, special clothing, vehicles, and breathing devices allow scientists to stay underwater to study aquatic life. Satellites collect images and other data from great heights above Earth's surface. Microscopes visualize objects that are too small for the human eye to see. Computers allow scientists to perform complex calculations with large amounts of data. Advances in engineering such as these have greatly changed scientific exploration.

Science Is Helped by Technology

Technology is all around us. It is needed in schools, homes, stores, and in communities. We all depend on technology. Scientific investigations are helped by many tools.

Glassware has many uses in the lab. Glass making is a very old technology. Earliest examples of glass date back to about 3000 BCE.

Digital scales are used to measure weight. Mechanical scales have been used for several thousands of years. Digital scales were first developed in the 1940s–1950s.

Light microscopes are used to see objects too small for human eyes to see. They were first developed in the late 1590s.

4. What are the basic scientific principles the engineers who designed the digital scales would need to understand to have this tool do its job correctly? Circle the correct answer(s).

   A. electric currents

   B. physical properties of metals

   C. influence of gravitational force on objects

   D. physical and chemical properties of materials used in building circuits

5. Identify two tools in the lab classroom, one that is used to measure volume and another that is used to observe objects. How would not having those tools affect your ability to carry out lab assignments?

Some Scientific Principles Important to Car Design

To build cars, engineers must have a strong understanding of science and math principles that relate to cars, such as:

 the anatomy and physiology of human body systems to design safe and comfortable interiors and exteriors.

 aerodynamics, including thrust and drag, to design sleek and efficient car bodies.

 energy transmission by waves for correct functioning of radio, interactive screens, and wireless software.

 forces and energy to understand the effects of gravity and collision forces on cars and on the materials they are made of.

Engineers Use Science to Solve Practical Problems

Imagine a team of engineers working to design a new car for a car manufacturer. The car has to meet certain safety requirements, meet the needs of the market, and not be too expensive to manufacture. Consumer safety laws require car makers to make safe cars for their customers. The engineers might like to build a car that can reach high speeds, and customers might like that too, but if the design of the car makes it dangerous it would never meet safety and environmental laws.

In order to evaluate different car designs and materials, the design team needs to apply knowledge of many scientific principles during the testing phase. Qualities such as the physical properties, chemical properties, and the strength of materials are tested. In this way, engineers depend on science to develop new technologies. Discoveries made by scientists can also inspire engineers. For example, carbon fiber was discovered by a scientist studying the physical properties of carbon. Carbon fiber is made of long carbon fibers that are woven together. It is light, strong, and resists high temperatures. These properties made carbon fiber suitable for use in cars and car parts.

Before a solution can be developed, the problem itself must be accurately defined. This can be done by identifying precisely what the solution needs to do. For example, the request that a car horn design be "loud" is not precise enough. "Loud" is not a quantitative value. However, "a car horn design that is 95 decibels" is a more precise design description that will help engineers develop a better product.

6. Use the word bank to complete the table by identifying the type of design concern that each question below addresses. Some of the questions may address more than one engineering concern.

Question	Engineering Design Concern
How can chemical pollutants emitted by the car be minimized?	environmental concerns
How can air conditioning and heating systems be added that are easy to use?	
How do different parts of the car withstand collisions?	
How can reliable wireless connectivity be added to the car design?	

Solve a Food Storage Problem

The modern canning process was developed in the early 19th century as a safe way to preserve, store, and transport food while minimizing spoilage. Canning was originally developed to feed an army, but it was quickly adapted for non-military purposes. Preserving food in a way that minimized the number of harmful microbes in it, that kept it relatively tasty, and that made it easy to store and transport was a need society had too, and canned food was an answer. Canned food remains fresh for much longer than fresh foods do. Before refrigeration was common, canned foods were in great demand as a way of keeping food at home. Modern canning is made possible by applying knowledge of many sciences, including biology, chemistry, and physics, to a real-life problem. Cans also created the need for another engineered object: the can opener!

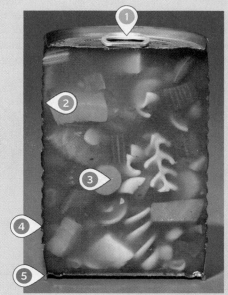

Canning technology has many parts

 Sealing the cans to make them airtight

 Making the cans tough enough to withstand knocks and bumps

 Heating the foods to high enough temperatures to kill harmful microbes

 Ensuring material from the can doesn't dissolve into the food

 Designing the lid and bottoms of the cans so they are easy to stack

7. Many modern can designs include a ring pull that allows the lid to be pulled off instead of needing a can opener to open it. What need might have led to such a design change?

_____

_____

_____

_____

Analyzing Influences on Technology

Technology helps people to meet needs such as food, shelter, and clothing in easier ways. The ways we communicate, play, and move from place to place are also shaped by technology. The bicycle is an example of a technology that has changed over time, for several reasons. Many bike design changes resulted from safety concerns, ease of use, or society's demands and needs. For example, societal changes such as the increasing independence of women led to the development of "safety bicycles." These bikes were designed to be safer and easier to ride than the large-wheeled penny farthings. The increased popularity of safety bikes caused a "bicycle craze" in the 1890s.

Influences on Bike Design

Today's bicycles are products of many changes over time. Each design change solved a problem that was present in previous designs.

1817

The earliest bicycles, such as the draisine, were made of wood and did not have pedals, brakes, a chain, or adjustable seats. They were designed to be propelled by the user pushing his or her feet off the ground.

1890s

Safety concerns about the awkward penny farthing led to the development of safety bicycles. These bikes had chains, gears, brakes, and air-filled tires, which allowed for easier steering and pedaling and increased comfort.

1960s–1970s

Increasing interest in exercise influenced the design of road bikes, BMX roadsters, mountain bikes, and commuter bikes.

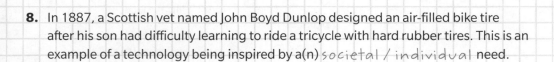

1870s

The penny farthing had a large front wheel and a tiny rear wheel. They moved when the rider pushed on pedals that were attached directly to the large front wheel. The seat of the bike was quite high off the ground. The bike did not have brakes. It was difficult to steer and pedal, and remaining balanced was difficult. Cyclists often fell off and got hurt.

Today

Materials technology has advanced so much that some bicycles are made of wood and bamboo — a return to materials the earliest bikes were made of!

8. In 1887, a Scottish vet named John Boyd Dunlop designed an air-filled bike tire after his son had difficulty learning to ride a tricycle with hard rubber tires. This is an example of a technology being inspired by a(n) *societal / individual* need.

Scientific Understanding Influences Technology

Scientific discoveries result in new kinds of technology. One modern example of this can be seen in the development of computer technology. Computing advanced rapidly in the 20th century. These advances were due to improved scientific understanding of such things as electric circuits and the physical properties of materials called semiconductors. For example, the components used to control the flow of electric current in computers are now much smaller and efficient than the large components used in the earliest computers. Over time, computers became smaller, faster, and more efficient because their components also became smaller, faster, and more efficient. Today they process data rapidly and can share data easily.

The earliest computers, such as this UNIVAC 1103, were very large and expensive. They were often the size of a room. They were mostly used by the government and military to perform complex calculations from large amounts of data.

Modern computers are thousands of times faster and have far more memory than the earliest household computers. Although the Internet was originally developed for scientists, people now use it for everyday activities.

9. Write one positive influence and one negative influence that computers have on society.

10. Write What would happen if every piece of technology around you were to disappear?

The Environment Influences Technology

The availability of natural resources has an impact on technology. For example, the manufacture of electronics relies on the availability of elements such as neodymium, aluminum, and silver. Some of these resources are found in very few parts of the world. Mining these resources has many social, economic, and environmental impacts. Some of these impacts are negative. Some engineers and scientists are looking into safer ways of mining the minerals. They are also investigating the use of other materials and the recycling of materials for use in electronics and other technology.

Society Influences Technology

Technology is everywhere. Technology is a necessary part of modern life. Humans have been engineering solutions to practical problems for a long time. The earliest forms of technology such as lighting fire, spears, cutting tools, and clothing helped people gather food efficiently and to stay warm. The basic needs for food, shelter, safety, and warmth influence the development of many technologies, and still do today.

Some modern technologies, such as snack foods, continue to be developed due to consumer interests or wants rather than needs. Consumer demand for watching movies on their phones has led to the design of phones with larger screens and the development of faster online streaming services. Many other technologies have been developed in response to changing attitudes and cultural norms.

For example, social awareness of the needs of people with physical disabilities has increased over time. Current laws require that schools, public transport, and living spaces be accessible to wheelchairs and other assistive devices. Such requirements have lead to the development of different assistive technologies such as chairlifts, showering benches, and assistive listening devices.

Laws that affect the mining and processing of materials can influence technology. Environmental laws such as the U.S. Clean Air Act and the Clean Water Act limit the amount of pollution that can be produced during manufacturing processes. Safety and health laws limit employees' exposure to hazardous conditions that could happen during mining or manufacturing processes.

Consumer demand for more interactive entertainment has influenced the size of TV screens and the development of smart TV technology.

Unvented gas space heaters were once commonly built into new homes. They have been banned in most U.S. states due to the risk of carbon monoxide poisoning.

Indoor bathrooms were once a luxury. Before the early 20th century, homes did not usually have toilets. People used outdoor toilets in small sheds called outhouses.

11. In the 1970s, the U.S. Environmental Protection Agency put limits on vehicle emissions because pollution from vehicle exhausts was linked to human diseases. As a result, car makers had to develop technologies that reduced pollutants in vehicle exhausts. What limit to technology does this situation represent? Check all that apply.

A. a social change that resulted in a natural change

B. a new technology that was informed by a scientific principle

C. a change in the law that resulted in society limiting technology

D. a technological change that resulted in a scientific discovery

EVIDENCE NOTEBOOK

12. Mosquito netting is often used in places such as Africa and South America where mosquitoes that spread serious diseases are found. Certain mosquito species, which carry diseases such as dengue fever, are spreading northward into cooler climates. Is netting a useful tool to protect people in colder places? Record your evidence.

Language SmArts

Identify Influences on Technology

Transportation is a vital part of modern life. But meeting the transportation needs of a community can be difficult. Extreme landscapes, rough terrain, and the need to preserve sensitive ecosystems all add to that challenge. Bridges, railways, and roads are transportation systems that require careful engineering. These technologies must meet complex environmental, physical, and societal needs, from minimizing the impact on the environment to maximizing the safety for users of the roadways. Civil engineers who design roadways consider factors such as material availability, motorist safety, and the effects of the structures and road system on wildlife.

The invention of different technologies influenced the design of roadways over time. Bicycles, asphalt, concrete, steel, cars, expanding business markets, and laws have all influenced the design of roads in different ways.

Dirt roads once connected many American cities. These paths, originally designed for traveling on foot, by horse, or by stagecoach, were simple to make and maintain, but could quickly become uneven, muddy, or dangerous.

Highways allow billions of vehicles to travel across great distances. Modern highway systems are also impressive feats of civil engineering. The U.S. highway system was one of the largest engineering projects ever built in the country.

13. Social, scientific, and environmental factors affected roadway technology throughout history. Based on your research, which of these factors likely had the greatest influence? Cite evidence, based on what you have read in this lesson to support your claim.

_____

_____

_____

_____

Assessing Impact of Technology on the Environment

Think about the materials that are needed to build computers and make packaged foods. All the raw materials for these technologies are taken from Earth. Raw materials are renewed over time by natural processes. Materials such as minerals take a very long time to renew, far longer than a human lifetime. In comparison, plant- and animal-based resources renew more quickly, over months or years.

Many foods available to you are products of technology. For example, wheat is used to make flour. After the wheat is grown, it is harvested, transported, and processed by machinery. The technology that makes the production and transport of food more efficient can also change the environment. These changes can have positive or negative effects on people and the environment.

14. Would collecting the resources that go into bread have long-term or short-term effects on the environment? Explain your answer.

Bread products are made of ingredients harvested from Earth. Flour, water, eggs, yeast, and milk are all grown or processed from natural resources.

Technology Uses Natural Resources

Natural resources are natural materials that are used by humans, such as water, minerals, and plants. Some natural resources are found all over Earth and others are found only in certain places.

Natural resources are taken from Earth in their raw form and processed to make many tools and objects. Taking resources from Earth can affect the environment. For example, wood is a material used in many engineered products. But clearing forests to harvest trees for wood removes habitats for plants, animals, and other living things. Mining for the minerals used in products such as electronic devices can affect the environment too. Mining can destroy habitats, erode the land, and release chemicals that can harm people and other living things. However, the harvesting and mining of resources also creates many jobs and businesses.

Neodymium is a rare-earth element. Its physical properties make it a good choice for use in tiny, powerful magnets.

Many of the raw materials found in electronic devices, such as neodymium, are mined from Earth. Before being used in products, these materials must be located, collected, and processed.

15. How is harvesting food crops similar to and different from mining?

Resources Around the World

Some resources are found all around Earth. Some others are found in a few places only. Some regions have conditions suitable for growing crops or trees, while other regions are rich in mineral resources. Environmental conditions influence the available resources.

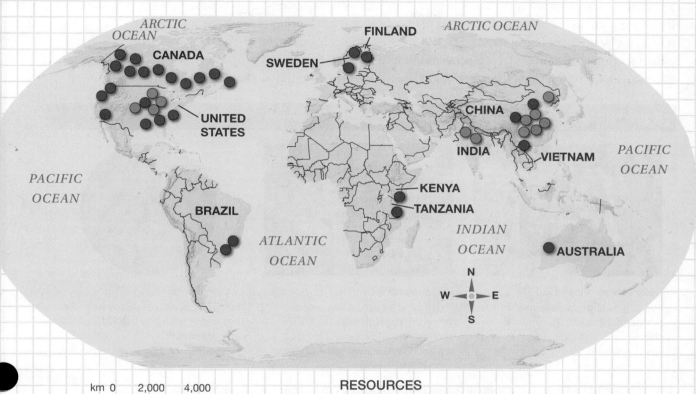

km 0   2,000   4,000

mi 0   2,000   4,000

RESOURCES
- Rare Earth Elements
- Forests
- Maize
- Wheat

16. Do the Math In 2015 approximately 734.1 million tons of wheat were produced globally. China produced the most wheat of any country, at 130.2 million tons. What percentage of the world's wheat yield did China produce in 2015?

17. Sweden is a heavily forested country in the northern hemisphere. The average tree coverage there is about 70%. Sweden is also a major exporter of wood products to the global market. Is the Swedish timber industry more likely a result of good resource availability or a lack of trees elsewhere on Earth? Explain your answer.

18. Each of the statements below describes a potential impact of the use of natural resources. Identify whether the impact has a short-term or a long-term environmental effect by circling the correct term.

Crops are harvested for food.   short term / long term

Resource collection methods are noisy.   short term / long term

Mineral resources are used up.   short term / long term

Technology Is Revised Based on Evidence

As scientific knowledge changes, so does technology. In some cases, engineers may adapt existing technologies based on new discoveries. Refrigeration is an example of a technology that changed with scientific discoveries. Early refrigerators used coolants that were harmful to humans. A new class of chemicals called chlorofluorocarbons (CFCs) replaced these harmful coolants. CFCs were a nontoxic improvement on the older technology. Scientists later discovered that CFCs damaged Earth's protective ozone layer. Current refrigeration technology has changed due to this evidence.

A Short History of Chlorofluorocarbons (CFCs)

CFCs were developed in 1928 by Thomas Midgley, Jr. as a safer refrigerator coolant than methyl chloride and sulfur dioxide, which were very toxic.

CFC coolants were nontoxic, making repairs and leaks less dangerous. When the coolant leaked out of the cooling system, it needed to be replaced, as is shown in the photo.

CFCs had an unintended side effect. In the 1970s, scientists discovered that they caused damage to Earth's ozone layer. Use of CFCs was banned and alternatives to CFCs were developed.

19. The use of CFCs was a response to the harm caused by the older refrigerants. What were some intended and actual effects of CFC use? Write your answers below.

	People	Environment
Intended effects		
Actual effects		

Analyze Resource Availability

The rare-earth elements neodymium and europium are needed to build electronics. They are found in only a few places on Earth and mining them can be expensive. So, recycling these elements from old electronics may help reduce the cost of making new electronics.

20. What other benefits of recycling these elements might there be?

_____

_____

_____

_____

Old electronics can be processed to recycle the expensive materials inside them.

Assessing the Impact of Technology on Society

Technology and Society Affect Each Other

The development of a technology does not guarantee its widespread use. A community's values and environmental conditions play a role in determining which technologies are developed and used. As shown below, identifying the effect of technology on society calls for an understanding of social and environmental factors.

Diagram of Water Supply Infrastructure

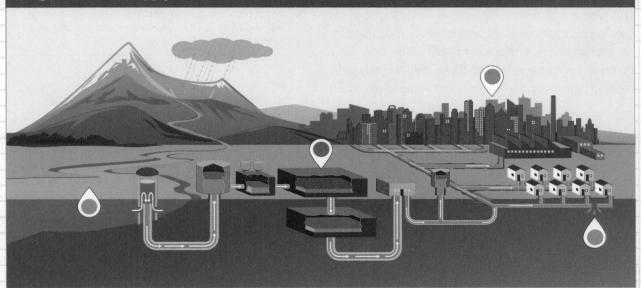

Processes for supplying water to a community can differ depending on the abundance and quality of water in the region.

People in a community may have different expectations of the water supplied to their homes. Is it safe? Is it free of harmful organisms? Does it contain harmful additives? These expectations may change over time, or vary from person to person.

Town and cities in dry or hot climates may have higher water needs than towns or cities in wet, rainy climates. For example, in dry climates, more water may be needed for growing crops and gardens.

The cost of repairing or replacing an existing water supply network is an important factor in maintaining access to clean water for residents. A technology is not useful to a community that cannot afford to purchase, maintain, or repair it.

21. How does climate most likely impact the water distribution system?

   A. If the area has a dry climate, water resources are likely to be limited or need to be pumped from farther away.

   B. If the area has a dry climate, people will need less water.

   C. If the area has a dry climate, the community cannot afford to replace cracked or rusted pipes.

   D. If the area has a dry climate, people in the community are more concerned about contamination of the water supply.

Technology Can Improve Quality of Life

Technology helps people accomplish everyday tasks. Technology allows people to travel by land, air, and sea, and to communicate with others all over the world. Medical technology has made many diseases easy to control or to cure. In the past, treatments such as controlling diabetes with medicine were thought to be impossible and organ transplants were experimental technologies. Today, they are both commonplace.

Assistive and adaptive technology plays a very important role in helping people in their daily lives. This type of technology includes devices such as hearing aids, wheelchairs, and titanium rods used to set broken bones. Other examples include devices that replace damaged or lost limbs, help keep hearts beating with a regular rhythm, and focus blurry vision.

The newest prosthetics have electrodes that connect to a person's nerves. These devices are controlled by the user's brain.

22. Identify the human needs that are addressed by the technologies listed in the table.

Technology	Issue to be addressed
hearing aid	
wheelchair	
glasses	
medicine	

23. Name two benefits that a modern electronic prosthetic device might have over an older, nonelectronic one.

EVIDENCE NOTEBOOK

24. Mosquito netting is most commonly used in developing countries. It is relatively cheap to make and is often distributed for free. What societal needs would demand that a tool be inexpensive to make or to buy? Record your evidence.

Hands-On Lab
Investigate a Technology Inspired by Nature

Throughout history, humans have developed many ways to make their lives easier. Many tools were invented by people who observed nature and realized that solutions to a human problem or need existed there. *Biomimicry* is the design and use of tools or solutions that copy natural structures or processes. For example, in 1941 George de Mestral, a Swiss engineer, noticed how seed burs got stuck in his dog's fur and in his own clothes. De Mestral was very curious about what made the seeds so "sticky." He viewed the burs under a microscope. What he saw inspired him to invent a type of clothing fastener he called Velcro. In this investigation, you will observe the structure of burs to see how it influences their function and how they inspired such a useful tool.

Cockleburs produce a fruit called a bur, which contains the seeds. Burs are covered in tiny hooks that attach to animals' fur, which helps disperse the seeds.

Procedure

STEP 1 Identify an engineering problem or a need for which a solution could be found in nature.

STEP 2 Obtain a bur and square of fun fur. Take turns observing how the bur sticks to the animal fur.

STEP 3 Observe the bur and the fur, using the magnifying lens. Describe their structure in the first column of the data table.

MATERIALS
- artificial animal fur (fun fur)
- cocklebur fruit (bur)
- hook-and-loop fastener
- magnifying lens

	Structure	Function
Bur and fur		
Hook-and-loop fastener		

STEP 4 Describe how the bur's structure affects its function in the second column of the table. Repeat Steps 1 and 2 while observing the hook-and-loop fastener.

STEP 5 Identify a design problem that could be solved by a nature-inspired solution.

© Houghton Mifflin Harcourt • Image Credits: ©Jim Lane/Alamy

Lesson 1 Engineering, Science, and Society   **19**

Analysis

STEP 6 Identify one or more natural objects, the structures and functions of which could be used to solve the problem or need you identified in Step 4.

STEP 7 What features of your chosen object or process make it suitable to solve the problem or need you identified?

Analyze the Impact of a Technology on Society

Some types of technology have had a greater impact on society than others. Agriculture is one area where technological advancements have had far-reaching effects. Agricultural technologies have increased the amount of food that can be grown per acre. Growing the same amount of crops but using less space means fewer existing habitats need to be disturbed to create farmland to feed an increasing human population. The areas of land that are being farmed are far more productive than they used to be. This is due to improvements in such things as plant breeding, soil preparation, harvesting, storage, and transportation.

Area Harvested and Production of Wheat in France from 1820 to 2010

● Production, in tons
● Area of land, in hectares

Source: Population and Development Review, 2013

25. From 1820 to 2010, the amount of wheat harvested in France decreased / increased / stayed relatively constant while the area of land use decreased / increased / stayed relatively constant.

26. The human population is projected to increase by 1 billion people by 2044. How will an increased demand on resources affect the need for agricultural engineering?

_____

_____

_____

_____

Continue Your Exploration

Name: _____   Date: _____

Check out the path below or go online to choose one of the other paths shown.

Designing an Efficient Lunch Line

- **Hands-On Labs** 👋
- **Careers in Engineering**
- **Propose Your Own Path**

Go online to choose one of these other paths.

In many situations, the solution to an engineering problem is not an object or tool, but a process or a system. For example, consider a cafeteria lunch line. A school lunch line is a process that is designed to serve meals to hundreds of people in a relatively short period of time.

Examine the Needs to Be Met

This is probably a familiar sight: the school cafeteria. Have you ever thought about all the steps that go into preparing and serving school lunches every school day? The food must be transported, prepared, cooked, and served. Ingredients must be monitored for freshness and nutritional content. And the meals should taste good too!

Define the Problem

Suppose that you've been challenged to engineer an improvement to your school's cafeteria. Think about the cafeteria as a system. Think about the key people, processes, and technologies that keep it running smoothly. Then, think like an engineer by asking specific questions that will help you identify the problem your solution will solve.

Continue Your Exploration

Developing Solutions by First Asking Questions

Asking very specific questions about the problem or issue you are trying to solve will help you identify the problem. Identifying the problem precisely will help you come up with more or better solutions. Asking questions will also help you identify the important and nonimportant factors of the problem. For example, asking "How many people use the cafeteria each day?", "What are the most popular meals and foods the cafeteria serves?", or "How long is the average wait for food on the busiest day?" will help you pinpoint possible problems that you can work toward solving.

1. What needs are not being met by a slow-moving or busy line at a school cafeteria?

2. Identify the people, processes, and technologies that play a role in the issue you identified.

3. Identify a factor that is unlikely to influence the length of time people wait in the lunch line.

4. **Collaborate** Serving several hundred people fresh, nutritious food every day in a cafeteria is a design challenge. How might nutrition science and engineering affect each other?

Can You Explain It?

Name: _____   Date: _____

Refer to the photo of the mosquito netting as you consider your answers.

What needs influenced the development of mosquito netting?

EVIDENCE NOTEBOOK

Refer to your notes in your Evidence Notebook to help you construct an explanation for how society and technology can influence each other.

1. State your claim. Make sure your claim explains how society's needs can influence the development of a technology.

2. Summarize the evidence you have gathered to support your findings and explain your reasoning.

Checkpoints

Answer the following questions to check your understanding of the lesson.
Use the photo to answer Questions 3 and 4.

3. What kind of need does this simple technology solve?

4. A positive / negative impact this technology could have on society is that it makes it easier / more difficult for people to get exercise outside by hiking.

Use the diagram to answer Questions 5 and 6.

5. What negative environmental impact(s) could occur during the building of this water infrastructure?

   A. release of pollutants into the water

   B. increase of precipitation in the mountains

   C. expansion of the water supply going downstream

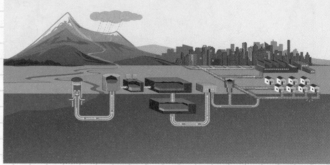

6. What positive impact(s) will the construction of this water infrastructure have on the town for which it is built? Select all that apply.

   A. provide a clean and reliable water supply

   B. decrease the precipitation in the mountains

   C. create more jobs for people in the town

   D. prevent the river from flooding

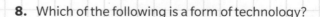

7. Another example of a technology is a toothbrush. Which of the following are important criteria for choosing the most suitable material for the bristles? Choose all that apply.

   A. The material comes in fashionable colors.

   B. The material is flexible and able to withstand wear.

   C. The material is able to support a large amount of weight.

   D. The material is nontoxic.

8. Which of the following is a form of technology?

   A. a lollipop stick

   B. a city park

   C. a public transit system

   D. a television

Interactive Review

Complete this interactive study guide to review the lesson.

Modern life is very dependent upon technology. Without engineered tools, scientists could not carry out research.

A. Explain how engineering and science are connected.

The use of technology is influenced by factors such as scientific discoveries, cultural values, and economic conditions.

B. Identify how scientific discoveries may influence the development and use of a technology.

Technology may have unintended impacts on the environment and people.

C. What is an example of the impact the use of a natural resource has had on Earth?

Small-scale and large-scale technologies can improve quality of life.

D. Give an example of how a large-scale technology such as agriculture has benefited society.

Systems and System Models

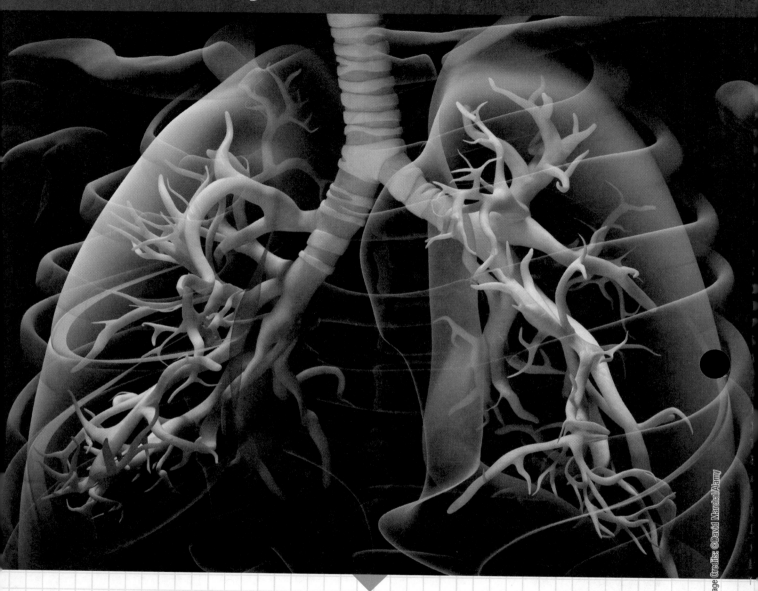

Computer models help scientists and engineers understand how systems, such as the respiratory system, work and how they are affected by changes to their different parts.

By the end of this lesson . . .

you will be able to describe natural and engineered systems and identify the role of system models in engineering and science.

© Houghton Mifflin Harcourt • Image Credits: ©David Marshall/Alamy

CAN YOU EXPLAIN IT?

How can weather be modeled to forecast the path and strength of a storm?

Scientists model the movement of air masses and forecast weather events using an understanding of weather as a natural system. Weather reports are based on models developed by scientists and engineers. People design and build engineered systems to solve problems.

Explore ONLINE!

1. Weather scientists collect large amounts of data about weather systems to build weather models. How might these models be helpful to the general public?

2. How might scientists' ability to forecast weather events, such as storms, be affected if they were unable to create models of those systems?

EVIDENCE NOTEBOOK As you explore this lesson, gather evidence to help explain how modeling systems can help engineers develop solutions.

Defining a System

A video game system includes game controls with computer graphics and sound. Your immune system helps your body fight disease. But what is a system? A **system** is a set of interacting parts that work together. Some systems are natural—they exist in nature. Other systems are engineered, or designed by people. Grouping a set of related parts or events together as a "system" allows scientists and engineers to study how energy and matter flow in nature. It also helps them study how an object's structure affects its function.

The Parts of a System

All systems are made up of parts, or **components**, that interact and carry out a process. Matter, energy, or information flow into, within, or out of systems. Matter, energy, or information that enters a system is called an **input**. A product of a system is its **output**. Both inputs and outputs can move across a system's boundaries. The output of a system or part of a system can be the input for another system or part of a system. *Feedback* occurs when the products of

This mini ecosystem is made up of red shrimp, algae, and coral enclosed in a glass sphere. The output of the algae returns as an input for the shrimp in what is called a *feedback loop*.

one system or part of a system affect another system or part of a system. For example, look at the mini ecosystem in the photo. A major input into the enclosed ecosystem is sunlight. Energy from sunlight is used by tiny algae in the water to make their own food. Algae make their food in a similar way to plants—using sunlight and carbon dioxide. This process is called photosynthesis. The algae release oxygen during photosynthesis. The shrimp take in the oxygen through their gills. The shrimp also eat the algae for food. Shrimp produce and release carbon dioxide during respiration. The carbon dioxide is used by the algae. It is all in a tiny system you can watch!

3. Outputs of one part of this ecosystem can be inputs to another. What are the inputs and outputs of the processes? Fill in the table with terms from the word bank.

WORD BANK
- carbon dioxide
- oxygen
- sunlight

Input(s)	Process	Output(s)
	Respiration	
	Photosynthesis	

The Respiratory System

The respiratory system interacts with other body systems. There are no real boundaries between systems in nature. But it is helpful to define boundaries so systems can be studied in isolation.

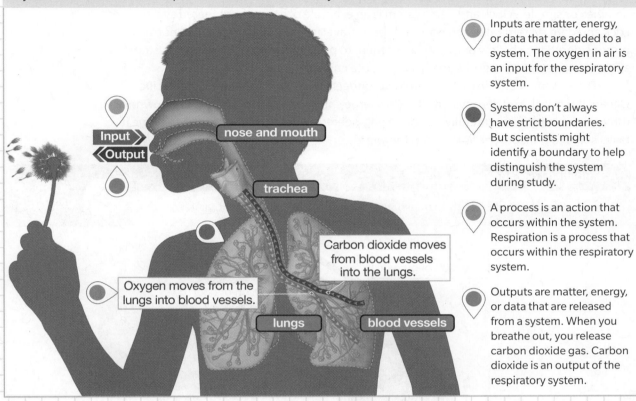

Inputs are matter, energy, or data that are added to a system. The oxygen in air is an input for the respiratory system.

Systems don't always have strict boundaries. But scientists might identify a boundary to help distinguish the system during study.

A process is an action that occurs within the system. Respiration is a process that occurs within the respiratory system.

Outputs are matter, energy, or data that are released from a system. When you breathe out, you release carbon dioxide gas. Carbon dioxide is an output of the respiratory system.

Input
Output

nose and mouth

trachea

Carbon dioxide moves from blood vessels into the lungs.

Oxygen moves from the lungs into blood vessels.

lungs   blood vessels

Natural Systems

During a checkup, your doctor might ask you to take a deep breath and exhale while he or she uses a stethoscope to listen to your chest. Your doctor is checking the health of your lungs, a part of your respiratory system. Your respiratory system enables you to breathe. It takes oxygen into your body. Your body's cells use the oxygen for important cell functions. Your trachea, lungs, and diaphragm are parts of this system.

The respiratory system is a natural system; it occurs naturally and was not designed by people. Natural systems often interact with one another. They do not operate alone in isolation. For example, breathing is controlled by the brain, which is part of the nervous system, and oxygen is carried by blood, which is part of the cardiovascular system. Natural systems do not have natural boundaries. A **boundary** defines the edges of a system and identifies the components of the system. Boundaries in a natural system are limits or borders, to the system that scientists and engineers define so they can study and model them.

4. Sometimes the respiratory system and the cardiovascular system (the heart and blood vessels) are grouped as one system called the cardiopulmonary system. How would the "regrouping" of two systems affect the components, boundaries, and processes of the new, larger system?

Engineered Systems

An engineered system is a system designed by people to carry out a task. Engineered systems can be as small as an integrated circuit or as large as a jumbo jet. They can be complex or simple. A lock and dam system is an example of a large engineered system. Lock and dam systems allow boats and ships to travel in waterways that would normally be considered too shallow or too steep for them to pass through. Lock and dam systems also allow vessels to travel upstream, against the current.

The Panama Canal in Central America connects the Atlantic Ocean to the Pacific Ocean. It has lock and dam systems to allow large ships to move uphill and then downhill through the canal. This carefully designed engineered system greatly reduces the time it takes ships to transport goods around the world.

A Simplified Lock and Dam System

This engineered system has solved transportation problems for hundreds of years.

 Explore ONLINE!

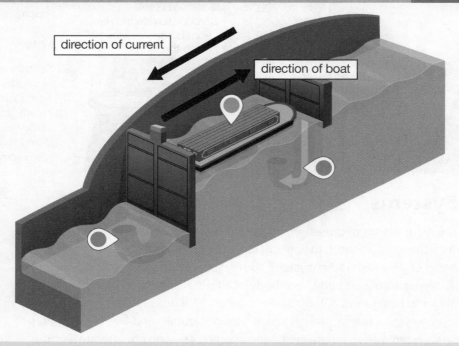

direction of current

direction of boat

A boat or other vessel enters the lock system when the gate is open. Once the gate is closed behind the vessel, water is pumped into the lock through the filling valve. This causes the water level in the lock to rise.

When a vessel is moving upstream, water is added to the lock by the filling valve to equal the upstream water level. This allows the vessel to travel upstream against the direction of the current.

Filling valves also release water from a lock to lower the water level. Lowering the water level in the lock allows the vessel to move smoothly downstream.

5. Fill in the blanks to best complete the following statements.

The lock and dam together form a _____ with _____ at the higher and lower river levels. Boats traveling through the lock start as a(n) _____ and end as a(n) _____.

WORD BANK
- system
- boundaries
- output
- input

Hands-On Lab
Investigate Components, Inputs, and Outputs of a System

Creating a simplified system will help you identify the relationship between components, inputs, and outputs within a system.

    With a small team, construct a model to investigate different parts of a system. You will identify how a model like this can help you understand processes within systems that have more components and processes.

MATERIALS
- flashlight
- safety goggles
- scissors
- shoe box
- tennis ball (or ball of similar size)

Procedure and Analysis

STEP 1 Carefully cut two large windows in a shoe box, as shown in the illustration. Your windows should be on opposite sides of the shoe box. The windows should be directly across from one another to create a clear line of sight between them.

STEP 2 Place the tennis ball inside the shoe box.

STEP 3 With the windows on the shoe box open, shine a flashlight through one window and out the other. You should see the light emerge on the opposite side of the shoe box.

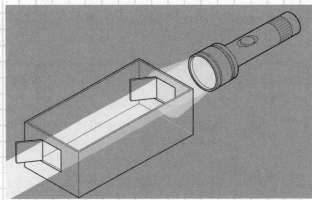

STEP 4 Experiment with the shoe box's window flaps and the tennis ball to find out under what conditions the light from the flashlight will be blocked or visible. Record your findings.

STEP 5 Identify the components, inputs, and outputs of your simple model system. Also identify the boundaries of the system.

© Houghton Mifflin Harcourt

STEP 6 Identify an interaction between two components that shows a cause-and-effect relationship.

STEP 7 What component(s) could you add to your system to change the light output?

EVIDENCE NOTEBOOK

6. Could a model representing the movement of air masses be built to forecast a storm? If so, what information would likely need to be included in such a model? Record your evidence.

Language SmArts
Summarize How Systems Thinking Is Useful

Many parts of the human body work together to allow breathing. So how do we know which components are part of the respiratory system and which ones are not? The answer is that people agree on the boundaries of natural systems. It is not always obvious which components are included until these boundaries are set and are agreed upon. Defining boundaries this way makes it easier to study them.

7. If the boundaries of natural systems are decided by people, why is thinking about natural systems useful? Review the content you have read so far to summarize why scientists find the concept of natural systems useful in studying nature.

Analyzing How Systems Interact

Systems do not exist in isolation. They are connected and can affect one another. For example, the human body contains many natural systems that work together to keep you alive. Smaller systems can be found within larger systems. Consider a cell phone. A cell phone is a small system that contains many tiny electronic systems, such as integrated circuits. Yet the phone itself is part of a larger communications system: a cellular network. A cell phone is of limited use if it cannot connect to other systems, such as other phones, within a cellular network.

A Simplified Cell Phone Communication Network

As you can see, cell phones are components of a large-scale engineered system. Cell phones themselves are made up of even smaller systems.

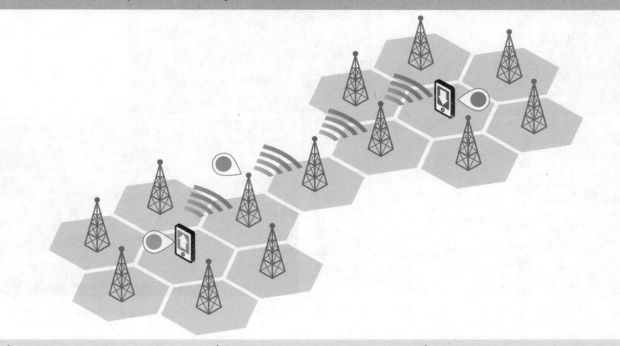

When a caller talks on a cell phone, a small microphone in the phone detects and converts the sound energy to electrical energy. The electrical signal is encoded in radio waves and sent to one or more base stations.

The radio-wave signal is sent to the base station nearest to the caller, and it eventually reaches the antenna of the receiving cell phone through one or more base stations.

The receiver's cell phone converts the radio signal it receives from the base station into sound energy, which is played through the cell phone's speaker for the receiver to hear.

8. The image above is a simplified model of a large, complex system. How might a simple model of a complex system like this be helpful in understanding how its components interact?

Natural System Interactions

When something goes wrong in a system, it can be challenging to discover the source of the problem. Systems are often interconnected with many other systems. Scientists and engineers study system interactions to understand how systems affect one another.

For many years, gray wolves were considered dangerous predators that threatened livestock and people in and around Yellowstone National Park. Wolves were killed to remove them from the area. In the 1970s, they were identified as an endangered species. Later, they were reintroduced in the park. Wolves became a new input to the Yellowstone ecosystem. They preyed on elk. This decreased the elk population. At the same time, the population of certain trees increased. Scientists concluded that the increase in tree population (a change to the system) was due to fewer elk eating the trees and saplings.

Wolves were removed from the Yellowstone ecosystem in the 1930s. In their absence, the elk population increased and overgrazed many plants.

Scientists noticed that the reintroduction of wolves resulted in an increased number of trees in the park.

More trees supported the growing populations of birds and beavers. Changes in one system can affect other systems.

9. If more wolves were added to the Yellowstone ecosystem, what effects would likely be observed? Select all that apply.

    A. The bird population would increase.

    B. The tree population would increase.

    C. The elk population would decrease.

    D. The wolf population would increase.

 EVIDENCE NOTEBOOK

    10. How does being able to understand the interactions of natural systems, such as weather, benefit society? How are the scientific practices of analyzing data and observation helpful in understanding how natural systems work? Record your evidence.

Do the Math
Explain Change by Examining Interactions

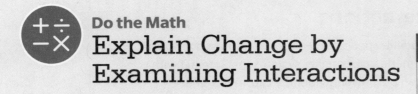

When scientists study interactions of natural systems, they are able to make predictions about how a change in one system may affect the components or inputs and outputs of other systems.

The scientific study of natural systems and how they interact can be applied to a variety of other systems such as weather forecasting, wildlife management, and medical treatments.

11. Which graphs show increases and which show decreases?

12. How do the graphs provide data about the effect of the elk population on the growth of aspens?

13. Imagine that wolves were never observed hunting and eating elk in Yellowstone. What then could you imply from the data showing a decrease in the elk population and the increase in the wolf population?

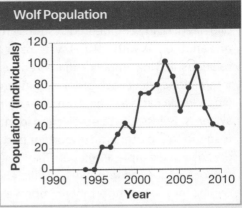

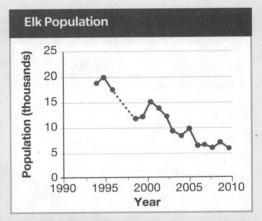

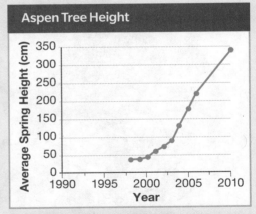

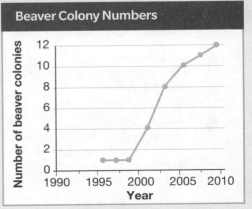

Source: Biological Conservation, 2011

Engineered System Interactions

Engineered systems are developed and built by people. They usually address a problem or a need. Many engineered systems are made up of smaller systems that interact with one another. As with natural systems, it can be difficult to identify cause-and-effect relationships in complex engineered systems. It is important to know how the system interactions affect each other so that larger, more complex systems can be developed if needed. A car is a large, complex engineered system that is made up of many smaller systems. Being able to predict and identify how those systems interact and how they respond to the user is an important part of developing a car or any engineered object or tool. For example, engineers may test engines and fuel systems to help reduce the rate of fuel use and improve fuel efficiency. Understanding how the fuel system and the engine interact is important to improving the interactions of the systems.

Four Subsystems of an Automobile

Understanding how the inputs and outputs of engineered systems affect system interactions is key to improving a system or developing new systems.

 Brake System
Is responsible for slowing or stopping the car when it is in motion

 Electrical System
Supplies electric current to many other systems in the car. Lighted panels and sensors rely on the proper function of the electrical system

 Drive Train
Uses forces from the engine to turn the wheels, causing the car to move

 Suspension System
Keeps the car stable by absorbing energy that could interfere with the forward movement of the car and it improves comfort and safety of the driver

© Houghton Mifflin Harcourt

14. Based on what you have read about car systems, which statements best describe how the suspension system affects the other systems? Choose all that apply.

   A. It reduces forward motion of a moving car.

   B. It provides energy for the electrical system.

   C. It reduces the amount of stress and strain on parts of the drive train.

   D. It prevents other systems from getting damaged by excess movement.

15. Systems, including cars, require an energy input. Where does the car, as a system, get its energy?

Predict the Effects of System Interactions

Systems are interconnected, changes in one system can have effects on other systems. Because of this, engineers usually do not study a single system in isolation. To really understand a system and to predict its behavior, engineers look at system interactions. They can then apply their understanding of system interactions to suggest and make improvements to the system. The system improvements may address an important problem or need of society.

16. Identify the inputs and outputs generated by the car as an entire system.

   A. Gasoline: input / output

   B. Gaseous emissions: input / output

   C. Energy as heat: input / output

17. **Discuss** Together with a partner, review how engineered systems can solve societal problems or needs. What real-world problems or needs does the car, as a system, solve? Identify one positive and one negative impact cars have on society and the environment.

	Society	Environment
Positive impact		
Negative impact		

Modeling Systems

As you have learned, systems and their interactions can be very complex. Scientists and engineers often rely on models and simulations to better understand and predict the behavior of systems. A scientific model shows the structure of an object, system, or concept. Simulations use models to imitate the function, behavior, or process under different conditions.

Engineers use system models to explore how a designed system works. They may also discover what might be going wrong in a system. Investigating a system model is usually safer, less expensive, and easier to study than carrying out investigations on the real-world system. For example, carrying out earthquake tests on scaled-down building models is much cheaper, easier, and safer than carrying out tests on a full-scale building.

Tests on scale models allow engineers to identify factors that make a system unstable. Potential problems with structural design or materials can be identified relatively easily.

18. Imagine you are a civil engineer who designs buildings. How might testing small-scale building models or their components be helpful in testing improvements and changes to the building design?

Different Models Meet Different Needs

Different types of models allow scientists and engineers to test ideas and find solutions to difficult questions. A physical model represents the physical structure of an object or system. Physical models often look and work like the object or system they represent. Mathematical models are models made up of numbers and equations. These models can often be shown as graphs and may be used to predict future trends. A conceptual or mental model is a way of thinking about how parts of a system are related in order to simplify complex relationships. Some computer models are like physical models in that they show the physical structure of an object. Other computer models are more like mathematical models.

The proportions, scale, and quantities used in a model must reflect the real-life object or system. For example, in modeling the piers and beams of a bridge, the scaled-down models must have the same proportions as the full-scale bridge. If not, the data collected while testing the model will not be valid. Models are also useful to run scenarios that would be impossible to do in real life, such as what may happen if Earth's temperature increased by 10°C.

© Houghton Mifflin Harcourt • Image Credits: ©Reuters/Issei Kato

Models and Simulations of Natural Systems

Scientists use system models to understand how natural systems work. The models help scientists develop explanations about natural phenomena that may be difficult to observe directly. Models are used to make predictions that affect our everyday lives. For example, meteorologists make weather predictions by using computer models based on collected weather data.

Models are very useful, but they have limitations. They may not work in the exact same way as the object or system they represent. This can happen if a model is studied outside of its natural environment. It is often impossible to account for every variable in a complex model. These differences can be accounted for when interpreting results.

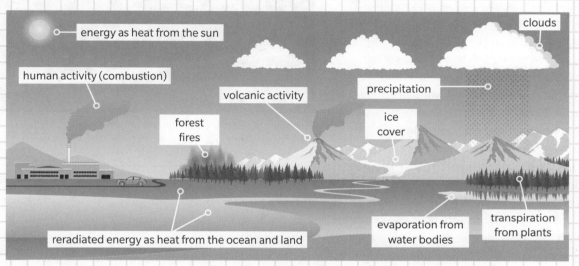

This diagram is a conceptual model showing components, inputs, and outputs of a climate system.

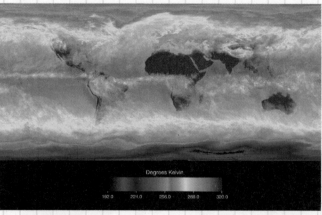

Computer models, such as this model of global air temperatures, can analyze data from many measurements and illustrate large-scale trends.

Complex systems, such as weather patterns or ocean temperatures, can be modeled by computers in a way that is easy to interpret.

19. What benefits does a computer model have over a physical model in the study of climate change? Select all that apply.

A. Computer models represent real-world objects.

B. The detailed study of climate does not lend itself to a physical model.

C. Computer models can be easily updated with collected climate data.

D. Computers can process data and trends in order to make climate predictions.

Models and Simulations of Engineered Systems

Engineers use models and simulations to analyze engineered systems. They test the models to see where flaws might occur or to test possible solutions to a new problem. Engineers also use them to test new ideas and to identify the strengths and limitations of their designs. Simulations can prevent costly and dangerous errors in design.

Imagine building an expensive rocket, and then launching it without knowing whether it would work. New rocket designs are first tested in simulations. Running a computer simulation of a rocket launch is much cheaper and more reproducible than using the actual object to test.

Models allow engineers to improve certain features or benefits of tools or processes and the systems that make them up. Engineers must have a good understanding of the mathematical relationships between system components. They may draw, label, and describe models to communicate issues and ideas with other engineers and scientists.

Engineers and designers often use physical models, such as this clay model of a car's exterior, to develop systems that work together.

Simulations may be used to show how an event might occur under specific circumstances. They allow scientists or engineers to test a hypothesis by changing certain conditions. Complex technologies can be tested in a variety of environments before they are put in use. During testing, design flaws may be found that can be corrected. This can prevent damage to an expensive piece of equipment or injury of people because of faulty design.

Step-by-step modeling during the design process helps engineers build a working product.

20. Review the statements about modeling the design and function of a motorcycle. Identify whether they describe an advantage or disadvantage of the model.

Engineered System Models	Advantage	Disadvantage
A computer model can illustrate properties that are difficult to observe directly, such as aerodynamic performance.		
A computer model does not account for every possible environmental factor.		
Physical models allow engineers to simulate dangerous events without the risk of human injury.		
A mathematical model of fuel used over time makes assumptions about the fuel use and the driving conditions.		

21. Do the Math | Collaborate Though models and simulations have many benefits, they are not "the real thing." Some factors or conditions must be approximated. Others cannot be reasonably included at all.

Imagine you are part of a group of engineers who need to test a scale model of a footbridge. It will be a $\frac{1}{20}$ scale model of the bridge. The footbridge will cross over a busy road and allow people to cross the road safely. How could a relatively small design error of 2 centimeters in the model system cause a significant problem in construction of the bridge?

EVIDENCE NOTEBOOK

22. When a computer model is used to forecast weather, the user must understand that the model cannot account for every variable that may exist in nature. Why is this important? Record your evidence.

Explore ONLINE!

Evaluate Benefits of Crash Testing

Seat belts and airbags are two technologies that have been demonstrated to be effective based on results in crash simulations. These simulations, or crash tests, use physical, full-size models of cars, drivers, and passengers. They are very expensive to conduct, so a lot of data is gathered during these tests to make them worthwhile. Automotive crash tests and the data collected from them have led to stricter safety guidelines for car manufacturers. This has reduced injuries in car accidents over time.

23. What are the benefits of crash-test simulations? Select all that apply.

    A. They do not put people in danger.

    B. They allow engineers to test new designs.

    C. The type and speed of the crash can be controlled.

    D. There is very little cost in performing the test.

24. What solutions would you propose to a car manufacturer if its car rated poorly in a crash test?

_____

_____

_____

Continue Your Exploration

Name: _____   Date: _____

Check out the path below or go online to choose one of the other paths shown.

Modeling Earth Systems	• Hands-On Labs ✋ • A Systems View of the World • Propose Your Own Path	*Go online to choose one of these other paths.*

Biosphere 2 is a structure built in Arizona as an experimental model of Earth's natural systems. It once contained living space, research facilities, and farmland. It also contained regions representing different biomes, such as desert and rainforest. People wondered whether something like Biosphere 2 could be used to support human life on Mars. In 1991, the first eight-member team began living in Biosphere 2 as a two-year project.

The physical structure of Biosphere 2 was an engineering success, but the biological projects inside the sphere did not go as planned. Several weeks of cloudy conditions led to reduced photosynthesis in the plants. The plants, therefore, did not take in carbon dioxide or release oxygen at expected rates. Bacteria in the nutrient-rich soils of the rainforest and savannah biomes broke down nutrients quickly. Most of the carefully selected pollinating insects died. This reduced the amount of fruits and seeds for the team to eat. These unexpected changes in the system inputs and processes affected oxygen and nutrient levels in the biosphere. As a result, the project was shut down. While the project did not achieve its original goals, the researchers learned many lessons about biological system interactions.

Biosphere 2 is now run by the University of Arizona as a research and conference center.

Continue Your Exploration

1. Biosphere 2 is an engineered system that was designed to be a closed system. In a closed system, energy can flow across the system boundaries but matter cannot. What type of energy transfers could occur in Biosphere 2?

2. Designers intended to use Biosphere 2 as a model for living quarters for people to live on Mars. However, several unexpected problems occurred. Even though the original project was not successful, what might researchers have learned from this "failed experiment"?

3. One unexpected problem that occurred was that excess carbon dioxide produced by soil bacteria was not used by plants. Instead, it reacted with concrete in the walls of the building and formed calcium carbonate. This chemical reaction "locked away" a large amount of carbon and oxygen from the organisms in the biosphere. Why is this a problem that might not have been predicted by studying natural ecosystems?

4. **Collaborate** Research the issue of excess carbon dioxide in Biosphere 2. Then work with a partner to create a poster-sized diagram showing the cause-and-effect relationships of increased carbon dioxide in a biological system. What type of designed system may have been helpful in this situation? Present your findings to your class.

Can You Explain It?

Name: _____   Date: _____

Consider how storm fronts such as the one in the photo can be modeled.

How can weather be modeled to forecast the path and strength of a storm?

Explore ONLINE!

 EVIDENCE NOTEBOOK

Refer to the notes in your Evidence Notebook to help you construct an explanation for how engineers and scientists are able to investigate and predict the behavior of a natural system.

1. State your claim. Be sure to tell how weather models may or may not help engineers and scientists predict the paths and strengths of storms.

2. Summarize the evidence you have gathered. Explain your reasoning. How does your evidence support your claim?

Checkpoints

Answer the following questions to check your understanding of the lesson.

Use the graph to answer Questions 3 and 4.

3. Choose all that apply. From this graph, you can identify

   A. a decrease in the elk component of the system.

   B. an interaction of the components of a system.

   C. an increase in system components.

   D. a decrease in food supply.

4. The graph shows a change in an ecosystem over time. What other information might you need before you can tell what caused the change?

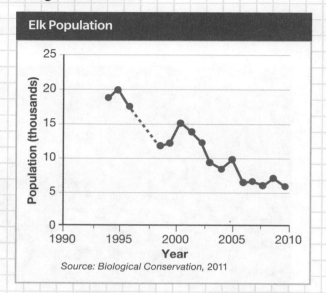

Elk Population

Source: Biological Conservation, 2011

Circle the correct answers in Questions 5 and 6.

Use the diagram to answer Question 5.

5. Identify each event as affecting an input, an output, or both in the vending machine system.

   A. the amount of change available in the machine:

   input / output / both

   B. not enough money inserted:

   input / output / both

   C. no product available:

   input / output / both

   D. the coin slot is blocked:

   input / output / both

   E. the counter is not counting inserted coins correctly:

   input / output / both

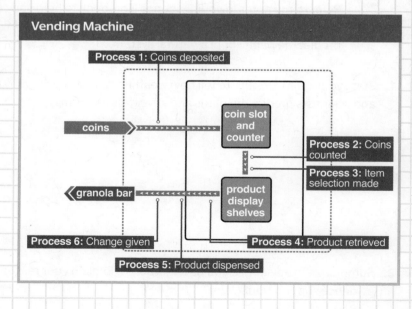

Vending Machine

Process 1: Coins deposited
coins
coin slot and counter
Process 2: Coins counted
Process 3: Item selection made
granola bar
product display shelves
Process 6: Change given
Process 4: Product retrieved
Process 5: Product dispensed

---

6. Engineers most likely use computer models / a full-scale model when designing a jet airplane. They do this to test the design of the plane and to identify how its subsystems interact. This type of modeling is done to observe how system components / outputs interact.

Interactive Review

Complete this section to review the main concepts of the lesson.

Systems are made up of interacting parts, or components.

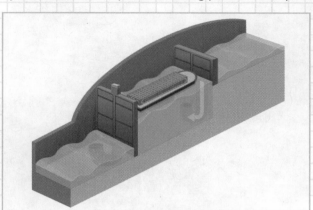

A. How are natural systems and engineered systems similar to one another?

Systems and subsystems interact. Studying system interactions is important in engineering and science.

B. In a complex system, many subsystems interact with one another. How do these systems interact in terms of inputs and outputs?

Computer models can be used to represent complex systems and their many interactions.

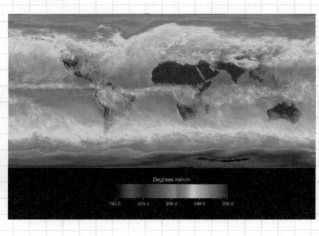

C. Why do scientists and engineers often use a model of a system to predict the results of interactions instead of studying the actual system?

The Engineering Design Process

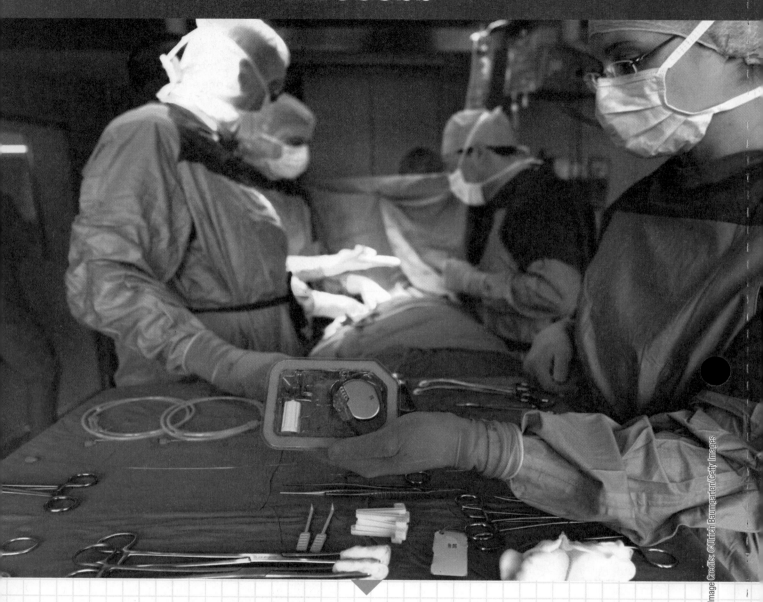

The function of the artificial heart pacemaker remains the same since the first one was developed in the 1920s, but its design has changed a lot.

By the end of this lesson . . .

you will be able to define the criteria and constraints of an engineering design problem in a way to ensure a successful solution.

Go online to view the digital version of the Hands-On Lab for this lesson and to download additional lab resources.

CAN YOU EXPLAIN IT?

How can the "need to have fun without causing injury" be stated as a design problem in building a safe and exciting wooden roller coaster?

Part of the excitement of a roller coaster ride is from the feeling of risk, but a ride that is too scary, too boring, or prone to malfunction would be unusable. How can a roller coaster design successfully meet the need for a fun, safe experience at the amusement park?

1. Imagine you are given the job of designing a wooden roller coaster for an amusement park in your town. What are some engineering and community-related issues you would need to consider before beginning the design process?

2. How might a lack of proper planning affect the design of a roller coaster?

EVIDENCE NOTEBOOK As you explore this lesson, gather evidence to help you analyze the purpose of engineering design processes.

Developing Solutions

You use many engineered objects every day. Each of them was designed and built to help with a need. Cell phone cases and roller coasters are very different devices. However, they are both developed using engineering design processes. Designing useful tools, devices, objects, and systems requires careful planning, testing, and manufacturing. The engineering design process has many steps. Although there is not a fixed order of steps, the design process for a cell phone case and a roller coaster are very similar.

Every Solution Begins with a Design Problem

Engineers solve problems. In order to design a solution, engineers must start with a clearly stated problem. In engineering, the word "problem" does not mean something that is wrong. Instead, an engineering problem is a statement that defines what solution is needed. The design problem must be stated in a way that tells what the solution needs to do and how it needs to do it. The problem being solved does not have to be complicated for an engineered solution to work. The chimpanzees below are not engineers, but they do have something in common with engineers. They were faced with a problem they needed to solve.

This chimp uses a stick to collect stinging ants from an ant colony so she can eat large numbers of them quickly.

3. **Language SmArts | Discuss** Together with a partner, look at the photo of the chimpanzee eating ants from a stick. Chimps, unlike humans, are limited to using nearby natural materials to make a tool to gather the stinging ants. In your own words, state the design problem faced by the chimp.

The Engineering Design Process

Engineering design has much in common with scientific practices. However, its purpose is different from that of scientific inquiry. The engineering design process involves defining and solving problems or needs. Engineers must define the design problem. They must identify features and qualities that a successful solution must have. Then they continue on in the engineering design process, which is shown in the diagram. Engineers do not always follow the design process steps in order. It is common for engineers to design a tool, object, or process, test the design, and find a problem with it. Then they go back to an earlier step to make a design change. It is normal for design changes to be made after testing.

An Outline of the Engineering Design Process

Testing and data analysis are parts of the engineering design process, because developing the best solution to a problem is based on analyzing data that indicates how well each design solution works.

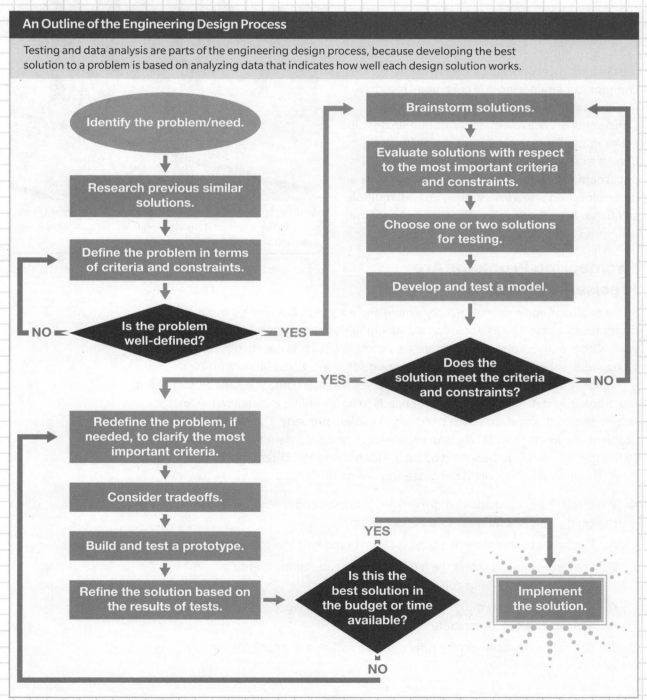

Define Problems and Identify Needs

The **criteria** of a design problem are the features or qualities the solution should have. Who needs the solution, what the solution should do, and how the solution will address the problem or need are examples of criteria. Other criteria may include requirements about ways the solution may affect society or the environment. When a design solution meets all criteria, engineers can compare several different solutions and evaluate which solution might work best.

The limitations that engineers face during the design process are called **constraints.** Some common constraints include cost, time, resource availability, laws, and scientific understanding. Constraints may have a quantity, or numerical value. For example, "the product must weigh less than 95g." If a design does not meet the constraints it is not acceptable. After the criteria and constraints are determined, engineers may come up with multiple solutions. They then evaluate how well each of the solutions solves the problem.

Comfort is one criterion for a helmet design. Riders are more likely to use a helmet if it is comfortable. The earliest helmets were made of padded leather strips.

Engineering Problems Are Precisely Worded

Some engineering problems are very simple and easy to define. For example, the thumbtack was created as a solution for attaching notes or posters to bulletin boards or walls. Other engineering problems are very complex, such as how to get around in busy cities. A city subway system is one engineering solution to this complex problem.

More complex problems need more time and analysis before engineers can define the problem in detail. It is important for needs to be identified in detail so the final engineered tool or system solves the design problem properly. The more complex the problem, the longer it will likely take engineers to precisely identify needs and criteria. Defining the problem to be solved by clearly identifying the criteria the solution must meet is an important step in the engineering design process.

4. Which statement provides a more precisely defined engineering problem related to designing a bicycle helmet? Choose all that apply.

   A. The helmet must prevent a bicyclist from being hurt in a collision.

   B. The helmet must protect the bicyclist from head trauma during a 30-kilometer-per-hour collision with a solid object.

   C. The helmet must reduce impact forces to the head when a rider falls from a moving bike onto a concrete surface.

   D. The helmet must shield the rider during a collision or a fall from the bike.

The Practical Need for a Bicycle Helmet

The idea of using a head covering to protect a bicyclist during a fall began more than a hundred years ago due to concerns about head injuries to riders. A fall from a tall, large- wheeled penny farthing could cause serious head and neck injuries. As more people began to ride bikes, more head injuries from falls occurred. It was a long time before helmets began to look like the ones you wear today. One of the earliest designs was made of simple strips of leather stitched together. While this design was comfortable to wear, it offered little protection to the rider. Bike riders also used motorcycle helmets, mountain climbing helmets, and construction hard hats. However, none of these helmets were designed specifically for the type of fall a bicyclist might have.

More and more injuries occurred for two main reasons. More people were cycling and riders were either not wearing helmets or were wearing helmets not designed for biking. Society needed a safety tool to help bicyclists protect their heads in falls from their bikes. A helmet designed specifically for biking conditions needed to be designed to provide protection.

Components of a Bicycle Helmet

The different components of a bicycle helmet are designed for specific purposes. They address the engineering problem of reducing the impact forces to a rider's skull from a fall or collision. Many components of a bicycle helmet have changed over time due to legal requirements and scientific research.

The shiny, flat covering on the outside of the helmet makes it look good. It also has a safety purpose. It reduces the frictional forces on the helmet that would occur if the expanded polystyrene shell was bare. The smooth covering reduces the possibility of the soft polystyrene interior snagging on a rough surface and causing a severe neck injury.

The expanded polystyrene shell provides protection by absorbing the energy of an impact. The foamy material absorbs the kinetic energy of the impact, collapses, and may crack. It also cushions the head from a very sudden deceleration that would happen if the skull were in direct contact with a hard surface such as asphalt or cement.

Fitting pads work along with the straps to keep the helmet stable on the rider's head.

A helmet that moves or falls off during a collision does not protect. Adjustable straps are needed for a good fit.

Do the Math
Calculate the Amount of Material Needed

Engineers can determine the manufacturing costs of a solution by calculating the amount of the materials that are needed to build it.

Explore ONLINE!

The airbag helmet was developed by design students Anna Haupt and Terese Alstin. It is made of nylon fabric that inflates when sensors in the collar detect a fall. Anna is showing how the collar is worn.

5. The collar that contains the airbag helmet is made of three pieces of fabric. The center piece is three times as long as the left piece. The right side is the same length as the left piece plus one quarter the length of the center piece. The lengths are cut end-to-end, from a single piece of fabric. How long must the fabric piece be if the left piece is 20 cm long?

Develop and Test Solutions

When it came to developing a bike helmet, many designs were looked at and tested. Some ideas worked. Some did not. The process of identifying what designs work and what designs do not is similar for all engineering design challenges.

After a design problem is defined, a team comes up with as many solutions as possible to the problem. Some ideas may seem silly. However, starting off with many solution ideas is better than starting with only one idea. Then each of the ideas are compared to see how well they meet the criteria and constraints of the problem. The ideas that meet criteria and constraints the best are kept. The other ideas are set aside. The most promising ideas are then rated. The rating is based on how well parts of each design meet the criteria and constraints. This rating step is helpful because some parts of a solution might be very successful. Other parts of the same solution might not solve the problem as well. If a single design idea does not address the problem well, the best features of each design may be combined into one best idea.

Consider Trade-offs

To work within the constraints of a design problem, engineers often make trade-offs. A trade-off is the act of giving up one design advantage in order to keep another. For example keeping costs low is important in any design project. However, using stronger, more expensive materials means the product is less likely to break and will last longer. For modern bike helmets, a light bike helmet design was preferred over a thicker, full- face covering design. Even though a thicker helmet that covers the face offers more protection, cyclists would be less likely to wear such a helmet because it would be heavier. Wearing a proper helmet offers much more protection than not wearing one does. Therefore, maximum protection was traded for a lighter design that more people would be more likely to wear.

6. Which of the following are examples of design trade-offs? Choose all that apply.

   A. the design of lightweight plastic materials to build car bodies to reduce weight and fuel use instead of using stronger, heavier steel which is more durable but will increase fuel use

   B. the design of larger wheels on mountain bikes to cycle more smoothly over rocky surfaces instead of smaller wheels that manage tight turns easier but cause a bumpier ride

   C. the use of a paper grocery bag to carry groceries home

   D. the use of lower quality, low resolution images in a phone texting program in order to be able send the images more quickly to a recipient

Optimize Solutions

After proposed solutions are selected and tested, the solution that performs the best in tests is chosen. Additional tests are done with this possible solution. A test model of the best solution is built and tests are carried out on this model. Design improvements are made to the model as a result of repeated controlled tests. For example, after repeated tests, the many-layered design of bicycle helmets was identified as the best way to protect bicyclists from head injury. Tests continued on helmet solutions to maximize bicyclists' safety. Tests were done to identify the density of foam that absorbs energy the best during a fall. Based on the test results, changes were made again to the helmet design. Its overall performance was improved due to this additional testing.

Design testing that is repeated many times is called **iterative testing.** The iterative design process involves testing, analyzing, and refining a product, system, or process based on test results. During the iterative design process, changes are made to the most recent version of the design based on test results. The purpose of the iterative design process is to improve the quality and usefulness of a design. The results of iterative tests help engineers develop the best solution possible.

EVIDENCE NOTEBOOK

7. Would it better to start the roller coaster design process by working with one design idea or four design ideas? Record your evidence.

Hands-On Lab
Design a Bicycle Helmet

Sometimes it is not possible to test a design by placing it in the actual situation in which it will be used. For example, you would not test a bicycle helmet design by having a person wear it in a collision and then checking the person for injuries. Instead, engineers often test a design solution using models.

You will design a bicycle helmet model and test it to see whether it meets the design criteria and constraints noted below. Your test helmet will be a small model of a bike helmet. You will test the model by dropping your helmet (open side up) with a raw egg inside. Observe the effects on the egg once dropped.

Your challenge is to build a helmet with these criteria and constraints in mind:

- The helmet will use only the materials provided to you.
- The outside width of the helmet will be no more than twice the width of the egg. Measure the egg's width at its greatest point.
- The helmet should protect an egg from cracking when dropped from a height of 1.5 meters (m).
- The egg must remain in the helmet during the test.

> **MATERIALS**
> - aluminum foil
> - bubble wrap packing with small bubbles
> - duct tape or reinforced strapping tape
> - egg (raw)
> - flexible foam sheeting
> - newspaper
> - paperboard strips
> - scissors
> - string or yarn
>
>

Procedure

STEP 1 Identify the engineering design problem based on the criteria and *constraints*. *Remember that criteria are the features the solution should have. Constraints are the limits designers have to work within. Which criteria or constraint might be the most challenging to meet?*

STEP 2 Identify three different design ideas that are possible using the provided materials. Sketch your ideas below or on a separate piece of paper.

© Houghton Mifflin Harcourt

56   **Unit 1** Introduction to Engineering and Science

STEP 3 Use the table below to evaluate how well you think each of your three designs meets the criteria and constraints. Use a scale of 1 to 3 to evaluate your designs. Then, based on the ratings, select one design. You may also draw the table on an extra sheet of paper.

Criterion or constraint	Evaluation of suggested solution against criterion or constraint
The helmet uses only the materials provided.	
The outside width of the helmet is no more than twice the width of the egg.	
The helmet protects an egg from cracking when dropped from a height of 1.5 meters (m).	
The egg remains in the helmet during the test.	

Analysis

STEP 4 Build your helmet using your chosen design. Then, test your helmet designs. Explain how each design relates to the design problem.

STEP 5 A large chicken egg weighs about 2 oz, or 56.7 g. A human head weighs about 10 lb, or 4.5 kg. In what ways might an egg be a good model for a human head in this design challenge? How might an egg not be a good human head model? Explain your answers.

STEP 6 Why was it necessary to have a precisely defined engineering problem before you started to develop and test a solution for your model helmet?

   A. The design problem was necessary to determine what materials are needed.

   B. The design problem was needed to define the criteria and constraints of the model.

   C. The design problem indicated what solution would most likely work when the designs were tested.

   D. The design problem measures the success of the solution after it is tested.

Define a Real-Life Design Problem

A working fire alarm can double the chances of surviving a house fire. Fire alarms generally attach to a ceiling. As a result, they can be hard to reach. Their loud, shrill sound can be very annoying, especially when the cause is burnt toast. However, these annoying aspects are actually important to the design. Because smoke rises, an alarm should be located high on a wall or ceiling to quickly and reliably detect smoke. The piercing sound may be needed to wake up sleeping people during a fire. The location and types of sound that are most effective have been determined by many years of research, testing, and analysis.

Fire alarms are designed specifically to sound shrill and annoying. Lives may depend on a fire alarm alerting people in the event of a fire.

8. It is important to define the criteria and constraints of a design problem to come up with a successful solution. Choose whether the following points are criteria or constraints. Place a check mark in the correct column.

Decisions	Criterion	Constraint
The alarm must produce a signal of at least 65 decibels at a distance of 10 feet.		
The battery compartment should be easy to open.		
The alarm should have a signal for alerting users that the battery is low.		
The alarm should weigh less than 225g (about 9 oz).		
The alarms must cost less than $3 each to make.		
The design should have as few moving parts as possible.		

9. **Write** In the space below, or on a sheet of paper, write down one other criterion or constraint that would be appropriate for a fire alarm design. Share your criterion or constraint with your classmates. Talk about how your ideas compare.

Comparing Engineering and Science Practices

Remember that science and engineering are related to one another. However, they have different purposes. Science is the search for knowledge about natural phenomena and how the universe works. Engineering is the application of science and math to solve problems. Technology uses both science and engineering to develop solutions to a problem.

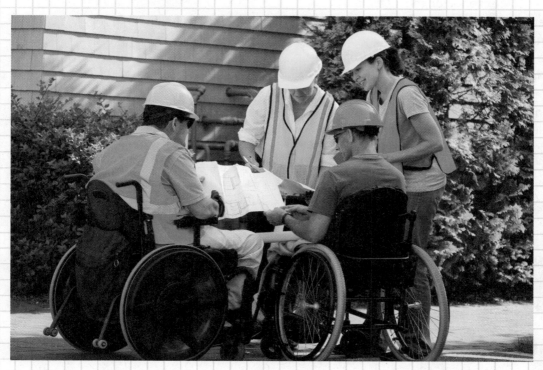

Engineers, like scientists, often work in teams with each member contributing specific skills and training. These engineers, in the white hard hats, are working with other team members on a construction site. Buildings, roads, and parks are all designed and developed using science and math.

Science and engineering practices involve investigations. However, the investigations have different purposes. In science purpose is to study natural phenomena and learn about how and why things work the way they do. In engineering, the purpose is to apply knowledge and build a useful device, system, or process. Both science and engineering use processes that depend on the results of tests and data analysis.

10. Read each of the following questions and decide whether it most likely would be asked by a scientist or by an engineer. Write your answer beside the question.

   A. What happens to growing plants that are exposed to low levels of ozone?

   _____

   B. What is the most effective glass thickness for a small greenhouse? _____

   C. What fuel-to-air ratio in a car engine produces the most power? _____

   D. What is the color of a solution of copper chloride in water? _____

   E. What is the minimum diameter of wire needed for a 150,000-volt transmission line? _____

Ask Questions and Define Problems

Scientists ask questions and seek answers in a systematic way. Engineers define a problem and look for a solution in a systematic way. For example, consider an investigation of tensile strength, the amount of force that a material can tolerate before it breaks. As a measured mass is added below the strip of material, the force exerted on the material increases. The material will stretch and eventually break. The amount of stretching and the force needed to cause a break depend on the property of the material known as *tensile strength*.

A tensile strength test could be used to investigate a science question, such as how the chemical properties of a material relate to its ability to withstand being pulled out of shape. The same test could be used to solve an engineering question, such as what material could be used to manufacture a part that must stretch less than 1% of its length when a certain-sized load is applied to it.

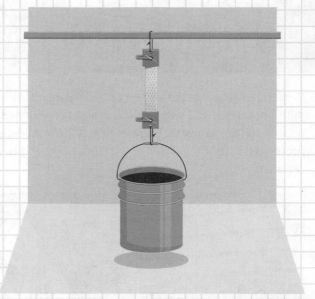

Tensile tests are commonly used to test how a material will react to pulling forces (forces being applied in tension). A strip of bubble wrap packaging is being tested to see how well the material withstands pulling and tearing.

EVIDENCE NOTEBOOK

11. What types of questions might be useful to ask when designing a safe and fun wooden roller coaster?

Develop and Use Models

In a scientific investigation, a model might be used to make a prediction. For example, a mathematical model might predict how a new material will stretch, based on its chemical composition and physical structure. A computer model of the atmosphere could forecast weather and climate changes. A physical model can show how atoms form molecules. Models are designed to account for many variables that affect the real life object or phenomenon, but cannot account for all variables. These differences are considered when analyzing data generated by the model.

Engineers also use models, but in a different way. Engineering models are generally built to test a solution to a problem or to determine whether a proposed solution will work. Models known as *prototypes* are often used to test a design. The prototype is a physical model. They are used to communicate ideas about design solutions to other people. Protoypes are also tested to improve the design of the solution. They can also be a smaller model of the object or a component of a larger object. For example, a prototype of a bridge part might be built and tested to find out whether it can withstand forces without stretching or breaking.

© Houghton Mifflin Harcourt

Plan and Carry Out Investigations

Planning an investigation is an important part of both science and engineering. In a scientific investigation, planning means asking a question, predicting a result, and determining a way to investigate the prediction. For example, a scientist may ask how chemical structure affects tensile strength, predict that certain types of chemical bonds will increase the strength, and then test materials based on the prediction. In an engineering investigation, planning means clearly defining a need and the criteria and constraints of the solution. For example, an engineer defines a need for an inexpensive packing material that does not stretch more than a certain amount under a specific load. During the planning process, it is determined whether the material is too expensive to be used in the solution. The engineer will only test materials that meet the cost constraints.

Strength testing of models is an important part of many engineering design projects.

Analyze and Evaluate Data

An important part of any science or engineering investigation is analyzing and interpreting data. The results of tests are useful only if they provide answers to questions or solutions to the problem. Results of tests often include measurements that provide data. This data is analyzed using math. Then it is evaluated to determine how the data relates to the prediction of the answer or the solution of the problem. For example, data from a tensile strength study can be analyzed and evaluated by plotting it as a graph. Graphing data like this allows an engineer to compare the amount of mass supported by the part to how much the material stretched.

 12. Do the Math This graph shows the data that students collected in a tensile strength test. In the first part of the graph, the curve is a straight line. This portion of the curve indicates elastic deformation of the material. If the weight is removed now, it will return to its original shape. In a later part of the graph, the curve levels out. This indicates plastic deformation. Applying this much force to the material changes the structure and causes it to stretch permanently.

Evaluate the data plotted on the graph. The point at which the deformation changes from elastic to plastic is called the yield point. That can be determined by identifying the point at which the stretch rate decreases. The mass at the yield point for this test is _____ .

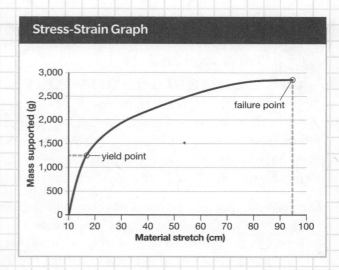

Construct Explanations and Design Solutions

Scientists and engineers use data for different purposes. Scientists use data to develop explanations of why or how something occurs. For example, they may relate the yield point of a material to its structure in order to explain how chemical bonds affect stretching. Engineers use data to design solutions. The yield point of a material determines how it can be used in an application where a force might cause a part to stretch.

Scientists and engineers need to clearly communicate their explanations and arguments when supporting a conclusion.

Engage in Argument from Evidence

Both scientists and engineers make arguments based on analyzed data. When the word *argument* is used this way, it does not necessarily mean that there is disagreement among people. Instead, an argument is a statement that explains something based on evidence collected. An argument may also tell about a solution that solves a problem. Data is used to support the argument. Data shows how the results match predictions or meet criteria and constraints.

Obtain, Evaluate, and Communicate Information

After results of an investigation or test are evaluated, they must be communicated clearly to be useful to other scientists and engineers. Data communication means clearly stating the results of the investigation, arguing that the results provide an explanation or solution, and supporting the conclusion with evidence. Other people should be able to use the communicated information to repeat the investigation and obtain the same results.

Language SmArts
Contrast Inquiry and Design Practices

Science and engineering both use a systematic approach to gather evidence. The main difference between these two areas is the purpose of the investigation. A scientific investigation answers a question or tests a hypothesis. An engineering investigation proposes and tests a solution to a specific problem in order to meet a need.

13. Consider your own experience in carrying out experiments. Also, consider what you have read about the purpose of tests in engineering and science. Compare and contrast the information you can get from reading about an experiment to the information you can get by carrying out that experiment yourself.

_____

_____

_____

Continue Your Exploration

Name: _____   Date: _____

Check out the path below or go online to choose one of the other paths shown.

| Careers in Engineering | • **Hands-On Labs** 👉
• **Earliest Examples of Technology**
• **Propose Your Own Path** | *Go online to choose one of these other paths.* |

Notice the structures that have been built in your town, such as roads, bridges, and buildings. Civil and mechanical engineers work on those structures. Civil engineers design and maintain public facilities including roads, buildings, railroads, and airports. Mechanical engineers design machines, such as elevators, that are used in these facilities. Civil engineers who work on using, improving, and restoring natural systems, such as rivers, seashores, and forests, are called environmental engineers.

Civil Engineering

Civil engineers are involved at every step of construction projects. They oversee project design and construction and maintain the project once it is complete. They use all the tools and steps of the engineering process from determining the engineering problem, defining its criteria and constraints, brainstorming new ideas, modeling and testing the ideas, and working on the final design. Then, they oversee the construction. There are many roles within civil engineering. Some of these include architectural, structural, and environmental engineering. Civil engineers also develop transportation systems and manage water resources.

Engineers from the Army Corps of Engineers inspect and secure a levee built across a roadway during a flood.

Continue Your Exploration

Army Corps of Engineers

While many people think of the Army as being involved in military activities only, the Army Corps of Engineers includes units that are trained for nonmilitary responses as well. Natural disasters can occur anywhere in the world. The U.S. Army Corps of Engineers has teams of engineers who respond to disasters in the United States and elsewhere. These teams are made up of engineers and other specialists who have the training and knowledge to deal with the effects of hurricanes, floods, earthquakes, and other natural disturbances that disrupt communities. Each team includes engineers who can lead missions, such as removing debris so that traffic can begin to move, providing emergency power, and assessing bridges and other structures to determine whether they are safe. The Army Corps of Engineers also helps perform search-and-rescue operations during disasters. They help find survivors who may be trapped and unable to reach safety on their own. Army Corps of Engineers team members include electrical, civil, transportation, structural, and hydrological engineers.

1. Which of these activities would likely include the work of civil engineers? Choose all that apply.
   A. designing a new sports stadium
   B. testing concrete formulas to be used in a parking garage
   C. brainstorming improvements to plastics used in making toys
   D. rebuilding severely eroded banks of a river to reduce flooding

2. Which of these activities would most likely include the job of a civil engineer who specializes in environmental engineering? Choose all that apply.
   A. testing steel beams for a large bridge
   B. brainstorming ways to prevent landslides on steep slopes
   C. designing a new system for unloading cargo from rail cars
   D. developing a robot to search for survivors of natural disasters

3. Explain why a response team that provides help after an earthquake would likely include many civil engineers.

4. **Collaborate** Identify one or more natural disasters in which engineers were involved in a community's recovery. Identify the roles that engineers had in restoring the functions of the community.

Can You Explain It?

Name: _____   **Date:** _____

Look at the photo of the elaborate wooden roller coaster as you consider your answers.

How can the "need to have fun without causing injury" be stated as a design problem in building a safe and exciting wooden roller coaster?

 EVIDENCE NOTEBOOK

Refer to your notes in your Evidence Notebook to help you construct an explanation of how the "need to have fun without causing injury" can be stated as a design problem.

1. State your claim. Make sure your explanation addresses why the criteria and constraints of the problem influence the design solution.

2. Summarize the importance of defining an engineering design problem, and explain how the criteria and constraints of the problem influence the design solution.

Checkpoints

Answer the following questions to check your understanding of the lesson.

Use the photograph to answer Questions 3 and 4.

3. Which of the items shown in the photo were developed using engineering design processes to develop a solution to a problem? Choose all that apply.

   A. computer

   B. coffee cup

   C. table

   D. pen

4. A laptop computer performs the same general functions as a desktop computer, but it is designed to address a different set of needs. Explain how the criteria and constraints of laptop and desktop design problems differ.

_____

Use the photograph to answer Questions 5 and 6.

5. An engineer proposes that a newly developed chemical could be sprayed from aircraft to slow the rate of burning in a forest fire. What is the next step the engineer is likely to take to develop a solution to fighting forest fires? Choose all that apply.

   A. Test a number of similar chemicals.

   B. Spray and compare the effectiveness of each tested chemical to water.

   C. Add the chemical to all aircraft spray tanks.

   D. Design a spray system for the chemical.

6. Scientists and engineers study the effects of fires. Identify which of these questions would most likely be asked by a scientist, an engineer, or both. Write S for scientist, E for engineer, or B for both.

   A. Which materials are best for fighting fires? _____

   B. How does turbulence above a fire affect aircraft that drop water on a fire? _____

   C. What percent of fires have natural causes? _____

   D. How does the type of terrain affect the path of fires? _____

Interactive Review

Complete this interactive study guide to review the lesson.

The engineering design process identifies a problem and then proposes, tests, and optimizes a solution to that problem.

A. Explain why testing a solution based on the criteria and constraints of the design problem is a key part of the engineering design process.

Science and engineering are related fields, but they have different goals and purposes.

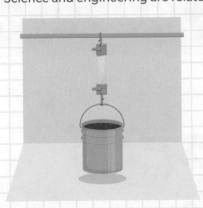

B. Models are important tools for both scientists and engineers. How do scientists and engineers differ in the way that they use models in their areas of study?

Choose one of the activities to explore how this unit connects to other topics.

☐ Health Connection

Cholera Today Cholera, an often deadly intestinal infection, has long plagued societies. In 1849 in London, England, cases of cholera were linked to bacteria from community water pumps. Pumping stations and sanitation throughout London were redeveloped as a result of these outbreaks. Today, the World Health Organization estimates there are roughly 1.4 to 4.3 million cases of cholera per year, resulting in 28,000 to 142,000 deaths worldwide.

Research a cholera outbreak and make a presentation about the causes of the epidemic. Describe what society and/or technology could do to prevent future outbreaks.

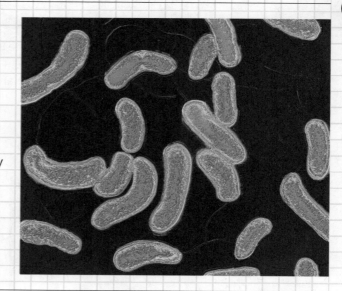

☐ Technology Connection

Biomimicry Biomimetics, or biomimicry, is the imitation of nature to solve human problems. Studying nature can help produce better human-made technologies and structures. In a recent example, scientists studied the ability of geckos to climb smooth surfaces. This phenomenon inspired NASA to develop a material with small synthetic hairs allowing it to remain sticky after many uses.

Research another nature-inspired technology. Use the research to create a poster, visual display, or electronic image that explains the technology. Present your findings to the class.

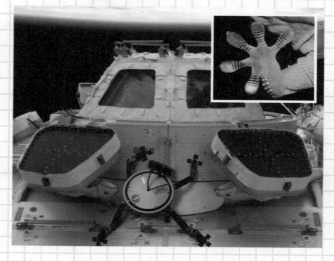

☐ Physical Science Connection

Catapult Design Catapults have long been used to launch objects using force. Variables including weight, force, speed, and distance must be considered when launching an object from a catapult. Engineers and scientists must master their understanding of forces in order to perform a launch successfully.

Research the design of a catapult. Create a multimedia presentation that combines text, sounds, and images to explain how a catapult works and is operated. Share your presentation with the class.

Name: _____   Date: _____

Complete this review to check your understanding of the unit.

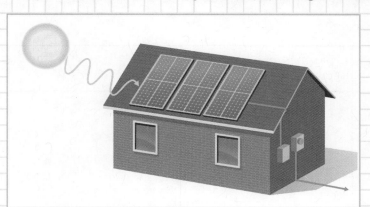

Use the image of solar panels on the roof of a house to answer Question 1.

1. Identify the components of the system.

The *input / output / boundary* of this system is sunlight.

The *input / output / boundary* is electrical energy.

Use the graph to answer Questions 2–4.

2. The graph shows changes in the populations of two species of aquatic organisms in Lake Michigan. What type of system does this represent?

A. a natural system

B. an engineered system

C. a functional system

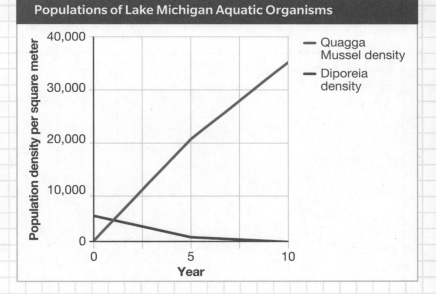

3. *Diporeia* is a shrimp-like organism native to Lake Michigan. The quagga mussel is an introduced species that was added to the lake. Which species could be considered new inputs to the system at the earliest time on the graph?

A. *Diporeia*

B. quagga mussels

C. quagga mussels and *Diporeia*

4. The amount of *Diporeia* in the system decreased as the input of quagga mussels increased. How might you increase the population of *Diporeia*?

A. increase the input of quagga mussels

B. decrease the input of quagga mussels

C. do not change the input of quagga mussels

© Houghton Mifflin Harcourt

Name: _____ **Date:** _____

5. Complete the table by providing at least one example of how these engineering and science topics relate to each big concept.

Engineering and Science	Energy and Matter	Stability and Change	Cause and Effect
Natural Systems	Energy and matter can be both inputs and outputs for natural systems. Plants convert energy input from the sun into matter output as new growth.		
Engineered Systems			
Human Impact on the Natural World			

Use the diagram of the pencil production process to answer Questions 6–9.

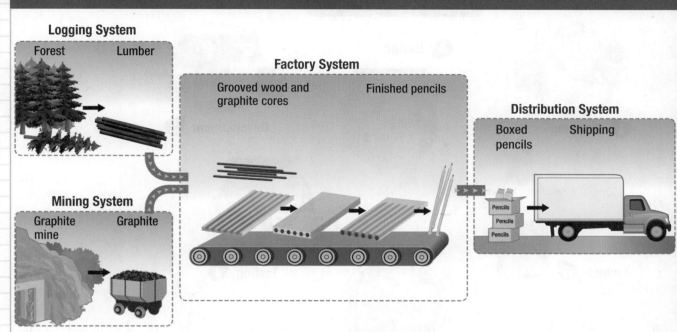

The Pencil Production Process

Logging System

Forest   Lumber

Factory System

Grooved wood and graphite cores   Finished pencils

Distribution System

Boxed pencils   Shipping

Mining System

Graphite mine   Graphite

6. Pencils are manufactured in a factory system. Based on the diagram, what are the inputs, outputs, and boundaries of this system during the production process?

7. What other systems outside of the factory are involved in the pencil production process? What are the inputs and outputs of those systems?

8. How do the inputs and outputs of the factory system relate to the inputs and outputs of the other systems? How would a decrease in the amount of available lumber affect the other components of the system?

9. The pencil is a device that has been improved over time through the engineering design process. How do a pencil's design features satisfy the criteria and constraints for a writing tool? How could it be improved?

Use the diagram of the web design process to answer Questions 10–12.

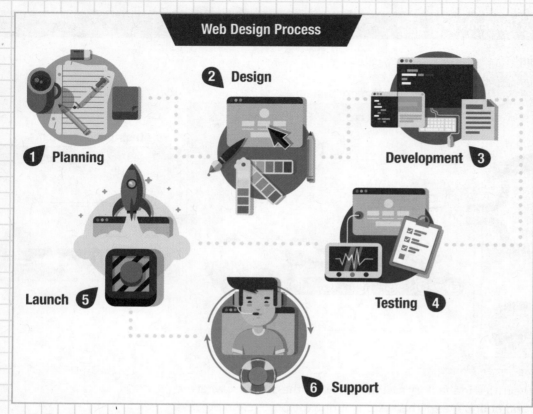

Web Design Process

1 Planning
2 Design
3 Development
4 Testing
5 Launch
6 Support

10. Recall the steps of the engineering design process. Compare and contrast the similarities and differences between the stages of the web design process and the engineering design process.

11. At what stage in the web design process are web designers most likely to return to planning with feedback for design improvement? What stage of the web design process most closely resembles the stage of the engineering design process at which the solution is implemented?

12. The engineering design process and the web design process both require the design teams to return to earlier stages and incorporate changes along the way. Why do these design processes involve multiple iterations of the design solution?

Name: _____   Date: _____

Which is the better water purification design?

The water supply for a town in a developing nation is not safe to drink due to bacterial contamination. Your team has been asked to evaluate two purification systems to provide drinkable water. Identify and recommend which design best solves the problem.

Gravity Filter

Filter Straws

In this design, gravity pulls water from a large clay tank through filters with tiny pores that remove bacteria. This design can be used to provide enough clean water for a family.

These tubes contain fibers that trap bacteria as water passes through. This design allows individuals to drink freely using suction as clean water passes through the fibers.

The steps below will help guide your research and develop your recommendation.

Engineer It

1. **Define the Problem** Write a statement defining the problem you have been asked to solve. What are the criteria and constraints involved in selecting a water purification method?

Engineer It

2. **Conduct Research** Identify possible societal and environmental consequences of each design solution. Describe the strengths and weaknesses of the solutions based on these factors.

3. **Evaluate Data** Analyze each design's ability to meet the criteria and constraints of the problem. Is one solution more useful than the other? Which purification method will help the most people in the community?

4. **Identify and Recommend a Solution** Make a recommendation based on your research. Which design should the town use? Explain your reasoning.

5. **Communicate** Present your decision to the townspeople. Your argument should use evidence that proves which design best meets the specified criteria and constraints as well as the strengths and weaknesses of the design. Describe a situation where the alternate solution may be more useful.

✓ **Self-Check**

		I clearly identified the problem along with criteria/constraints for this problem.
		I researched design solution strengths and weaknesses.
		My solution is based on evidence gathered from my research.
		My recommendation is clearly communicated to others.

The Practices of Engineering

This rocket car was developed and engineered for optimized speed. Each year people gather in Black Rock Desert, Nevada, to watch cars similar to this break the world land-speed record.

Engineers apply scientific knowledge to perform research, design solutions, and then optimize their designs. The practices of engineering are used to develop and improve technologies such as solar, electric, recreational, and even aquatic cars. In this unit you will learn about each phase of the engineering design process and engage in process yourself.

Why It Matters

Here are some questions to consider as you work through the unit. Can you answer any of the questions now? Revisit these questions at the end of the unit to apply what you discover.

Questions	Notes
When have you seen the design process applied in a real-world situation?	
What decision-making tools do you use in your everyday life?	
When have you had to redefine a problem or redesign a solution in your life?	
What examples of design optimization do you see in your neighborhood?	
Why is it important to define a problem clearly and precisely?	
How does brainstorming with others help to find better solutions?	

Unit Starter: Identifying Criteria and Constraints

Criteria and constraints are important to consider when defining problems and needs. Consider the invention of the beep ball. It allows people with vision impairments to play baseball or catch. In this game, the ball has a beeper. The players listen for the beep in order to catch the ball.

1. Identify each decision point by writing either *criterion* or *constraint* on the line.

   The ball should produce a beep of at least 50 decibels. _____

   The ball should run on a 9V battery. _____

   The ball should cost no more than $10 to produce. _____

   The ball should weigh between 100 and 200 grams. _____

   The ball should comply with consumer product safety standards. _____

   The ball should have a 16-inch circumference. _____

   The ball should be able to turn on and off. _____

 Go online to download the Unit Project Worksheet to help you plan your project.

Unit Project

Off to the Races

Competing teams need a reliable way to race their boxcars. Plan a method to test boxcars for speed and durability. Then design a track that will minimize friction and maximize the speed of the cars while keeping them aligned on the track.

Defining Engineering Problems

Trebuchets were medieval weapons designed to hurl objects weighing 100 kilograms a distance of up to 300 meters. Their design was based on the sling.

By the end of this lesson . . .

you will be able to explain the importance of precisely defining engineering problems before developing solutions.

Go online to view the digital version of
the Hands-On Lab for this lesson and to
download additional lab resources.

CAN YOU EXPLAIN IT?

How does the purpose of a treehouse affect how you would design and build it?

Before you start to build a treehouse, you have to figure out what structural design will allow it to
serve the purpose you need it to, as well as what resources you have available to you.

1. What are some questions that you might need to ask as you plan and design
   your treehouse?

2. Is "having access to a tree" an important factor in planning and building a
   treehouse? Why or why not? Explain your answer.

EVIDENCE NOTEBOOK As you explore the lesson, gather information to help
explain how defining design problems precisely helps engineers.

Solving a Design Problem

Engineers use scientific principles and knowledge to address practical problems. The engineering process begins when a problem, need, or desire is identified. Scientists and engineers work to develop and design a solution to the problem. Engineering problems can be as small as designing a new type of pen or as large as designing and building a spacecraft to explore Mars. The solution can be an object, a process, or even a system involving many tools and processes.

Indoor open fires release harmful products such as soot and carbon monoxide into the air. People in the home then breathe these in, which can cause diseases.

Engineering Begins with a Problem, a Need, or a Desire

A situation that often leads to serious health problems in developing countries is how people cook food and warm their homes. In much of the developing world, people cook food over open fires or open stoves inside their homes. These stoves are usually poorly ventilated, which causes the fuel to burn incompletely. The fires and stoves do not usually have a chimney or stovepipe to remove smoke from the home. People who live in the house are exposed to smoke and gases from the fires. Gases, smoke, and soot from the fires cause illness and lead to the death of millions of people each year. There is a need to find practical ways to decrease this harmful exposure. Millions of lives could be saved each year. This is an example of a need that could be solved through an engineering solution.

3. **Discuss** Describe the problem in the photo as it relates to health issues. Consider how that problem could be addressed by the development of a tool or object.

© Houghton Mifflin Harcourt • Image Credits: ©John Lund/Stone/Getty Images

Questions Help Define the Engineering Problem

To develop a solution, the engineering problem must first be carefully defined. Engineers ask questions about the need. Then they conduct research to help form a precise definition of the engineering problem. For example, the widespread use of open fires and open stoves in the developing world leads to millions of deaths each year from exposure to smoke and combustion gases. This large-scale health problem can be addressed only by precisely identifying the parts of the social and physical systems in which the problem or need occurs. Questions that help to develop a solution will also identify the systems in which the problem exists, including:

- the individuals or groups that need the problem to be solved
- the scientific issues relevant to the problem
- potential impacts of solutions on the environment and society
- the cost-effectiveness of the design process and availability of resources
- the economic realities of the people for whom the solution will be developed

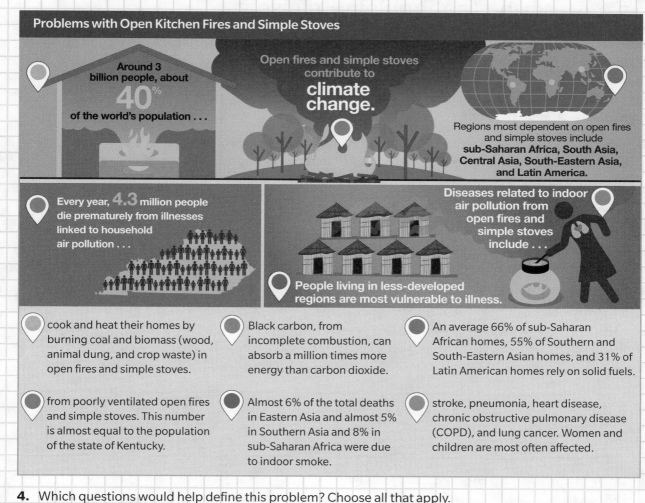

Problems with Open Kitchen Fires and Simple Stoves

Around 3 billion people, about **40**% of the world's population . . .

Open fires and simple stoves contribute to **climate change.**

Regions most dependent on open fires and simple stoves include **sub-Saharan Africa, South Asia, Central Asia, South-Eastern Asia, and Latin America.**

Every year, **4.3** million people die prematurely from illnesses linked to household air pollution . . .

Diseases related to indoor air pollution from open fires and simple stoves include . . .

People living in less-developed regions are most vulnerable to illness.

cook and heat their homes by burning coal and biomass (wood, animal dung, and crop waste) in open fires and simple stoves.

Black carbon, from incomplete combustion, can absorb a million times more energy than carbon dioxide.

An average 66% of sub-Saharan African homes, 55% of Southern and South-Eastern Asian homes, and 31% of Latin American homes rely on solid fuels.

from poorly ventilated open fires and simple stoves. This number is almost equal to the population of the state of Kentucky.

Almost 6% of the total deaths in Eastern Asia and almost 5% in Southern Asia and 8% in sub-Saharan Africa were due to indoor smoke.

stroke, pneumonia, heart disease, chronic obstructive pulmonary disease (COPD), and lung cancer. Women and children are most often affected.

4. Which questions would help define this problem? Choose all that apply.

A. How do open fires in homes cause health problems?

B. What types of buildings usually have kitchens with open fires?

C. What treatments are available for diseases caused by open fires and stoves?

D. What is the household income of families with open fires in the home?

5. **Draw** The engineering problem related to open indoor fires can be represented as a system. Illustrate the problem of open indoor fires as a system. Don't forget to add the components, processes, inputs, and outputs of this system.

 Language SmArts

Describe the Problem Precisely

Suppose you want a new smartphone application that lets you quickly add a caption to a picture before you send it to friends. Software engineers work on this type of design problem. This is a smaller scale problem than redesigning how millions of people around the world cook and heat their homes. Even so, the problem needs to be described in detail before designing a solution.

6. In the table, each stated problem identifies a smartphone need or desire. The precisely stated problem gives further detail about the engineering problem, which then guides a designed solution. Fill in the blank sections of the table with details that address a more specific need or desire from that of the stated problem.

Stated Problem	Precisely Stated Problem
Develop a phone that can be used by adults with special needs.	Develop a phone to be used by vision or hearing impaired persons.
Develop a phone that is more "eco-friendly."	Develop a phone that contains at least 25% recycled materials.
Develop a phone that has a camera.	
Develop a way to protect a phone from damage.	
Develop a phone that is affordable.	

Defining Problems Precisely

If an engineering solution is to be useful, the problem must first be defined precisely. Imagine designing an umbrella to keep someone dry while they are walking in light rain. Your umbrella design must address the need that the umbrella stops rain from falling on a person's head. It must also allow the person to carry other things at the same time. With these needs in mind, design criteria might include that the umbrella must be light. Therefore, the umbrella must be made of lightweight materials and materials that are waterproof. The criteria that define this umbrella design do not necessarily apply to all umbrella designs, though. Think about how criteria for a shade umbrella or an umbrella that can stand up to hail might be different.

Umbrellas and other rain gear must all meet specific needs of the users to be useful.

7. Which of these requirements are things you would need to consider when designing an umbrella that will keep an elderly person dry in rain showers? Choose all that apply.

A. fabric that is water repellent or waterproof

B. colorful fabric print

C. fabric that you cannot see through

D. lightweight materials

EVIDENCE NOTEBOOK

8. How would the precisely stated engineering design problem of a treehouse to be used by six-year-old children be different from that of a treehouse to be used by teenagers? Record your evidence.

Specific Needs and Limitations
Define Engineering Problems

Lighted city streets are much safer than dark streets. Until gas lamps were developed in the late 18th century, oil or kerosene lamps were used to light up streets and pathways. Then gas-fueled lights improved upon those lamps. However, gas lamps caused fires and explosions. In addition, the light from these lamps was not bright enough to light large areas. Many gas lamps were then replaced by carbon arc lights. These lights used a glowing carbon electrode that made the light very bright. They were placed high above street level. Unfortunately, arc lights needed a lot of work to keep them lit.

The invention of the incandescent bulb improved the technology of outdoor lighting. Both streetlights and traffic signal lights used these bulbs. Today, streetlights and signal lights often use light emitting diodes (LEDs). These are more energy efficient. They last much longer than incandescent bulbs. Each new streetlight design was developed to meet the changing needs of people. In addition, changes to design have been made as more resources become available.

Many criteria of the engineering problem of lighting up city streets have not changed in more than 100 years. Streets still need to be "brightly lit." However, today's constraints may be very different.

Criteria

Engineers must know the criteria for a solution before they begin designing a solution. The solution should meet most of the **criteria**, or the requirements set out when defining a problem. Criteria include: who needs the solution, what the solution should do, and how the solution will address needs. Solutions may meet some or all criteria. For example, the criteria "must be cheap to make" and "must be made of strong materials" may be met by some or all proposed designs. Some designs might be cheaper to make than others. Some designs may include stronger materials than others. Engineers then decide how important each criterion is for a successful solution. They compare designs and see how well they meet each criterion. This process is called making trade-offs. For example, a streetlight design that is made of strong materials makes the light safer and less likely to break. However, it will be more expensive to make.

Constraints

The limits on the design of a solution are called **constraints**. Constraints are often expressed as having a value or limit, for example, "It cannot cost more than $10 to manufacture", or "It must withstand the force of a car crashing into it at 55 kilometers per hour." Constraints can also be limiting factors that exist because of such things as the availability of raw materials, the laws of physics, or current scientific understanding. If a proposed design solution does not meet the constraints, it is unacceptable or unusable. For example, when incandescent lightbulbs were invented, they were not immediately used in streetlights. They could not be used until a system to provide electric energy to city blocks was developed. The absence of a reliable energy source was a constraint. Other constraints include time limitations, cost of materials, and environmental concerns. Precisely defining the criteria and constraints of the problem increases the success of possible solutions.

9. Imagine you are designing streetlights for your town. The table below lists the criteria the solution should address. Number the criteria in order of importance to your design problem so you can design the best street lighting. Compare your order of criteria with your classmates. Discuss reasons for the order of your criteria.

Criteria	Order of Importance
The lights should light up all areas of the street.	
The lights should be cost-effective to run.	
The lights should not shine into drivers' eyes.	
The light poles should be made of strong, sturdy materials.	
The lights should be made of environmentally safe materials.	
The lights should be of vintage style to match town buildings.	

10. Street lighting was originally developed to improve public safety. Rate the importance of the criteria listed in the table as they relate to public safety concerns. Explain your reasoning.

Redefine Criteria and Constraints

What happens if you change the problem? When you do that, you need to define new criteria and constraints. This cyclist is trying to stay dry in the rain using an umbrella. Think about the criteria and constraints that were used to design a rain umbrella. The umbrella was a good design solution. Does the same solution work for keeping a rider dry while cycling? Think about how to define the criteria and constraints of this problem. The solution should keep a rider dry and safe while cycling in the rain.

11. Suppose you are leading a design team that is working on ways to keep cyclists dry in the rain. A standard rain umbrella creates some safety concerns. Your first task is to make a list of at least three criteria and three constraints that will help your design team to state the problem before they begin developing a solution.

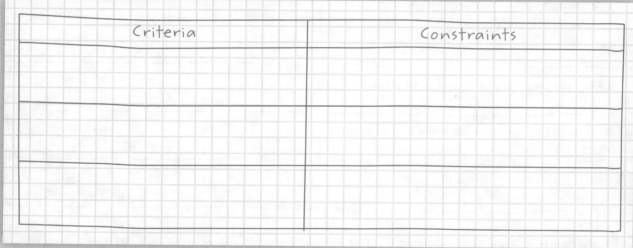

Criteria	Constraints

12. Write a precisely defined engineering problem for a design solution that protects a bicycle rider from the rain. Use the criteria and constraints that you identified above.

_____

_____

_____

_____

_____

_____

Researching to Define Engineering Problems

Soapbox car racing, also known as gravity racing, is an annual event in many places in the United States. In these races, sleek, motorless cars race downhill. Drivers race against each other or against the clock. The cars do not have engines, but they can reach speeds of up to 56 kilometers per hour (35 miles per hour). Gravity racing events began in the mid-1930s and were open to male racers only. Since 1971, female drivers also race. Anyone between the ages of 7 and 20 years old can compete in these annual races to build the fastest car. The challenge for participants to build the fastest car possible is a good example of using scientific knowledge to precisely define an engineering problem.

Imagine that you have entered a soapbox car race. You will use the engineering design process to state the engineering problem and then design a solution.

13. Research will help you identify how this problem was addressed in the past. Your goal is to make the fastest car along the given course. First, identify questions you need to answer to precisely define the design problem you face. Then, identify the information and data you will need to plan the next steps of the design process.

The design of soapbox cars, also called gravity racer cars, has changed over time. The availability of different materials and safety concerns are just two influences on the design.

Questions to Answer	Information and Data Needed

Engineering Problems Can Be Reframed

An engineering question builds on initial research. Sometimes, though, new information may require engineers to change, or reframe, the engineering question. This new information may mean that the question needs to be restated and a new solution proposed.

When Criteria or Constraints Change

Reframing may be needed when there is a change in the criteria or constraints of a problem as well. For example, after your research on the soapbox car, you might find out that cars are scored on appearance as well as speed. This new criterion requires that you reframe your question. A new constraint, such as a change in the maximum width of the car body, means your design question needs to be reframed. Your design problem now has different dimensions that affect the amount of materials needed.

Reframing an engineering problem in the early stages of the solution development is better than doing so later, after the testing phase begins. Defining the engineering problem so that it best describes the problem without having to consider time or cost would be ideal. But, it usually does not work that way. Engineers need to research production costs, schedules, market pressures, new scientific discoveries, and customer likes and dislikes before they can clearly define engineering problems. This type of research helps identify the criteria and constraints for a successful solution.

These wooden derby cars look different from one another, but they all were designed to meet the same constraints and criteria to make the race fair.

14. After you start planning the design for your soapbox racecar, you find out that the maximum weight for the car has changed. What new information do you need and what changes to your design plan would you have to make in order for your design to fit the new constraints?

 EVIDENCE NOTEBOOK

15. Imagine that the materials with which you planned to build the treehouse roof were now too expensive for you to afford. Would it be necessary to reframe your engineering problem? Record your evidence.

© Houghton Mifflin Harcourt • Image Credits: ©Lynn Seeden/E+/Getty Images

Hands-On Lab
Design a Model Car

Building a soapbox car is an exciting engineering project. You can re-create the steps of the box car design process by building a model car in class over several lessons.

Your challenge is to build a model car that will travel the farthest after being rolled down a three foot long ramp slanted at 30°. In developing a solution, you need to think about how limits such as the materials available to you, the time you have to complete the solution, and scientific principles will affect the available solutions.

The first step is to define the engineering problem using the criteria and constraints the solution must meet. The criteria and constraints that define your design problem are:

- The mass of the car must not be greater than 120 g.
- The length of the car must not be greater than 15 cm.
- The width of the car must not be greater than 7 cm.
- The car must have a 4.5 cm distance between the axles.
- The car must have a 1 cm clearance underneath the body.
- The car must be made only from materials provided by your teacher.
- The car body may have any shape and be attractive.
- The car must be reusable.
- The car must have four wheels.
- The axles, axle housing, and wheels supplied with the kit must be used.
- The axles, axle housing, and wheels may not be changed in any way.
- The only weights that may be added to the car are washers supplied in the kit.
- A to-scale model driver, made from paper, may be added to the car.

MATERIALS
- corrugated cardboard
- wooden wheels (4)
- wooden axles (2)
- smoothie straws
- Metal washers (weights)
- tape
- scissors
- measuring tape
- digital balance scales (per classroom)

Procedure

STEP 1 Criteria are features the solution should have. Constraints are the limits the designers need to work within. What are the criteria of this design problem?

STEP 2 Identify the constraints of the design problem.

STEP 3 Clearly state the design problem. What is the need that is being met by this design problem?

How is this model car similar to a soapbox car? How is it different?

Analysis

STEP 5 **Do the Math** As part of your design, you want to cut out a paper driver to attach it to the top of your car. You want the driver to be correctly scaled to the car as if it were a soapbox derby car. The length of a typical soapbox derby car is 1.2 m. Your model car is 14 cm long. To the nearest centimeter, how tall should your model driver be in order to represent a 1.67 m tall driver?

STEP 6 Why is it important to define the design problem more precisely than "design a small, fast model car"? Explain your answer using what you have learned about the engineering design process.

Redefine an Engineering Problem

If the race rules were changed to say that each car should have three wheels instead of four, you would need to redefine the problem. Your design would have to include changing the locations of the wheels and changing the car's weight distribution.

16. Suppose a student wanted to use the same car design in a new competition. She discovers the rules are different. For each new rule, match the letter that indicates the type of influence that rule will have on her model car design.

A. Change to criteria
B. Change to constraints
C. Change in materials list

_____ The car must have a 2 cm clearance below the body.

_____ Plastic wheels or rubber wheels may be used on the car.

_____ Cars will be judged on appearance and performance.

Continue Your Exploration

Name: _____   Date: _____

Check out the path below or go online to choose the other paths shown.

Redefining
a Design
Problem

• **Hands-On Labs** ✋
• **Learning from Design Failures**
• **Propose Your Own Path**

Go online to choose one of these other paths.

Wind is a renewable energy source because it is generated continually. Wind turbines use wind to produce electrical energy. In many places around the world, giant windmill-like turbines stand on top of ridges, in wide prairies, or offshore. In these fairly isolated places, the structures do not generally interfere with the lives of people. These large turbines are not designed for use in a urban areas because they take up a lot of space and require strong winds to move their blades.

Adjustments for Societal and Environmental Needs

How could you use engineering design to develop a way to harness wind energy in a city while meeting the constraints of urban needs? One solution is the Wind Tree shown in the picture. This artificial tree has "leaves" that are lightweight wind turbines. Generators and cables are located inside the branches and trunk. The Wind Tree silently produces electric power even in a light breeze.

French entrepreneur Jérôme Michaud-Larivière developed the design after observing how even a very light wind rustled the leaves on trees. Michaud-Larivière wondered whether a wind-energy device based on several mini spinning turbines could generate enough energy to be useful in cities. The Wind Tree design has a relatively low power output of about 3.1 kW from light breezes when compared to the 2.5 to 3 mW output of traditional, large, land-based turbines. Michaud-Larivière suggested that a street lined with Wind Trees could power city streetlights or help offset the power use of nearby buildings.

Continue Your Exploration

1. Explain, in terms of criteria and constraints, why the design of a traditional wind turbine might not be suitable for use in a city.

2. For the mini turbines to work properly, which of the following criteria are important in choosing the material to make them from?

   A. Lightweight

   B. UV resistant

   C. Recycled

   D. Realistic leaf colors

   E. Attracts insects

   F. Rustproof

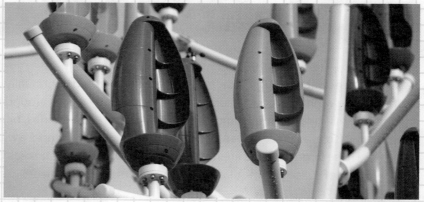

The "leaves" of Wind Trees are miniature turbines. They can move in light breezes.

3. **Do the Math** The kilowatt (kW) is a measure of power. Wind Tree turbines have a power output of 3.1 kW. The lightweight leaf turbines can move in light breezes. A traditional, large wind turbine can have a power output of up to 3 megawatts (mW), but strong winds are needed to move the large turbines. The large turbines are more powerful machines than the smaller Wind Trees because they can do the same amount of work over a shorter period of time.

   How many Wind Trees would it take to match the power output of five large turbines? Round your answer to the nearest whole number.

4. **Collaborate** As a team, learn about how changes to environmental and health laws and concerns have changed the definition of engineering problems that engineers of city infrastructure and energy-harnessing technologies deal with in the world today.

Can You Explain It?

Name: _____   **Date:** _____

Examine the photo of the girl building a treehouse as you consider your answer.

How does the purpose of a treehouse affect how you would design and build it?

EVIDENCE NOTEBOOK

Refer to the notes in your Evidence Notebook to help you define the engineering problem of building a treehouse.

1. State the design problem. Make sure the problem is stated clearly and precisely.

2. Summarize how identifying the criteria and constraints allow you to define the engineering problem.

Checkpoints

Answer the following questions to check your understanding of the lesson.

Use the photo to answer Questions 3 and 4.

3. The ladder for this treehouse has been removed because the wood was rotting. You need to design a new way to get into the treehouse. Which questions would help define this engineering problem? Choose all that apply.

   A. How much do the users of the treehouse weigh?

   B. What materials and tools can I use?

   C. Is the rope on the tire swing strong enough to be safe if two people are on the tire?

   D. Is there a way to close the window for privacy?

4. Each statement below refers to the engineering problem of designing and building a new way into the treehouse. In the blank cells of the table, classify each statement as a criterion, a constraint, or neither a criterion nor a constraint of the problem.

Availability of tools and boards	
Desire to remove treehouse access after entry into it	
Maximum height of the treehouse above the ground	
Availability of roofing materials	

Use the photo to answer Questions 5 and 6.

5. The candles in the photo are a solution to a well-defined problem. What problem do these candles solve?

6. One hundred fifty years ago, the solution illustrated in this photo was the best solution to the need to provide light at night. Today, it is not the best solution to the same engineering problem. What has likely changed so that candles at a dinner table now meet a different need?

Interactive Review

Complete this interactive study guide to review the lesson.

An engineering design problem defines a solution that will address a human need or want.

A. Why is it important to identify the right questions when developing a solution to an engineering design problem?

In order to develop a usable solution to a design problem, the problem must state specific needs and limitations that must be met.

B. How are criteria and constraints used to make a precisely stated solution to an engineering design problem?

Researching how similar problems were addressed in the past can help engineers define the design problem precisely.

C. Sometimes an engineering problem must be reframed. What might occur that would require an engineer to reframe an engineering problem?

Developing and Testing Solutions

Thomas Edison did not invent the incandescent light bulb, but he did improve its design and make it more practical.

By the end of this lesson . . .

you will have learned about the practice of developing and testing solutions to engineering problems.

Go online to view the digital version of
the Hands-On Lab for this lesson and to
download additional lab resources.

CAN YOU EXPLAIN IT?

How would you develop and test ways to get your kite out of a tree?

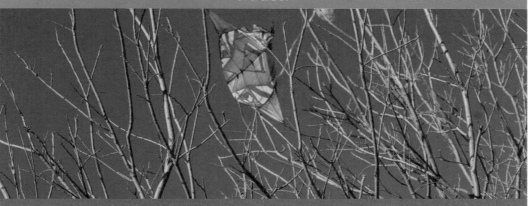

Oh no! Your favorite kite is caught in a tree and its string is tangled in the branches. What can you do to free it? A workable solution is one that keeps you safe and keeps the kite and tree as intact as possible.

1. Distinguish between the criteria and constraints of this problem. Remember that constraints are the limits that a solution must remain within. If a solution violates a constraint, it must be removed as an option.

2. How could you develop and test possible solutions to the engineering problem of safely getting the kite out of the tree?

 EVIDENCE NOTEBOOK As you explore this lesson, gather information to help you develop solutions to an engineering problem.

Developing Solutions

There is not always one clear solution to an engineering problem. After the criteria and constraints of a problem have been defined, engineers often brainstorm ideas for solutions. Often, several possible solutions meet the criteria and constraints of the problem. Each solution is tested to determine which one best meets the criteria and constraints of the problem.

For example, your class is planning a field trip to study a stream ecosystem. Part of your study includes analyzing the water quality of the stream using probeware similar to that shown in the photo. Eight sets of probeware will be used by the class. It is not possible to drive directly to the stream, so you need to carry the equipment from the school bus. The distance from the bus parking lot to the stream is a quarter mile. Defining this transportation problem using criteria and constraints and then prioritizing the criteria will help develop a solution.

After identifying the important requirements of the problem of transporting testing equipment to the stream, brainstorming and planning help develop solutions.

3. Using a scale of 1–5, identify the importance of each criterion of the transportation problem.

	Rating (1-5)
Must be easy for a student to use, carry, or hold	
Must not damage the electronic equipment	
Must be reusable	
Must be inexpensive	
Must not be damaged by being used on a rocky trail	

4. **Discuss** Before the field trip, your class discusses the best ways to move the equipment. One student suggests using the janitor's hand-pulled, metal wagon. You test this idea and discover that the equipment would get scratched if placed on the metal bottom of the wagon. What could you do to address the issue with scratching?

Brainstorm Solutions

One way to generate ideas is to brainstorm the problem with other people. When you work with others to think about and generate ideas quickly, you are **brainstorming.** You can brainstorm in different ways, but the most important thing is to suggest as many ideas as possible while avoiding judgments about any suggestions. The goal of a brainstorming session is to identify many solutions in order to find a few to refine further. Some ideas may end up unusable, but brainstorming is not the time to figure out which ideas may or may not work. Brainstorming many ideas can often result in a much better solution than starting with a single idea alone. Not considering more than one option from the start can limit the creativity of the solution.

Brainstorming sessions can generate a lot of ideas.

5. One of the goals of brainstorming is to generate a number of possible solutions. Which statements are advantages of brainstorming many ideas instead of focusing on one initial solution? Choose all that apply.

   A. Multiple ideas increase the chance of finding a workable solution.

   B. Larger groups can reach a conclusion about a solution faster.

   C. Several different ideas might combine to form a better solution.

   D. New ideas may be generated off of others' suggestions.

The Importance of Being Open-Minded

All ideas are considered valuable during brainstorming sessions. The ideas proposed in a brainstorming session are not completely random, though. As possible solutions are suggested, it is important that the criteria and constraints are kept in mind. One very important constraint for any solution is the budget. A solution such as using drones to carry the equipment to the stream is not a workable solution. It would be too expensive for the school to afford. On the other hand, if each student already had their own drone they could bring with them, using drones might be a workable solution. When brainstorming, participants also have background knowledge about how similar problems were solved in the past. They can also use what they know of scientific principles and laws related to the problem and the proposed solutions. For example, there are several laws that restrict the use of drones. If the use of drones is prohibited in the area where the field trip is, then they are not a suitable solution even if the school could afford to use them.

The Importance of Background Research

In order to find the best design solution for an engineering problem, research is also needed. If you jump straight into brainstorming without researching solutions that are already available, or how similar problems were solved in the past, you do extra work and waste time. Part of the solution may already exist. By researching the problem, you start with a background of knowledge. Sometimes background research helps reframe the problem so that it is better focused. Research into a solution often continues after ideas are generated by brainstorming.

Use Decision-Making Tools

Some of the brainstormed solutions may not meet all the criteria of the problem, or maybe all of the solutions meet the criteria. Some solutions may be more effective or safer than others. Possible solutions are evaluated against the criteria and constraints. Less-effective solutions are rejected, and the remaining solutions are refined.

Workable solutions must meet the constraints of the problem. If a solution does not meet a constraint, it is eliminated. For example, renting a satellite phone to send data home from your field trip would be beyond your budget. But for a research team in a ship on the ocean, a satellite phone might be the best option to stay in contact with others.

Decision Matrix

Several decision-making tools can help you choose among the solutions to find the best option. A **decision matrix** is one tool for evaluating several options at the same time. In a decision matrix, a number is assigned to a criterion that rates its importance in a successful design solution. For example, "does not leak" is the most important criterion in the decision matrix below. It was given a rating of five points. The higher the points, the more important the criterion is to a successful solution. Each solution is then scored on how well it meets each criterion. Points are awarded for each solution up to, but no more than the maximum rating given to the criterion. The result is a numerical ranking of the proposed solutions. The solution that has the highest score is the one that best addresses the problem.

This decision matrix evaluates the proposed solutions for taking soup to school for lunch. The criteria of the problem were ranked according to how important they were for a successful solution. The highest scoring solution is the plastic container with the screw-on lid.

		Solutions			
Criteria	Criterion rating (1–5)	Plastic container with screw-on lid	Foam container	Glass jar with lid	Plastic zipper bag
Easy to reuse	4	4	2	3	1
Does not leak	5	5	3	4	2
Not expensive	4	2	4	1	4
Unlikely to break	3	3	2	1	1
Totals		14	11	9	8

6. Which solution meets the criteria the best? Explain how the matrix provides useful information for evaluating the solution to the problem.

EVIDENCE NOTEBOOK

7. Should you identify whether each proposed solution exactly meets the criteria and constraints of the problem when you brainstorm solutions to get the kite out if the tree? Record your evidence.

Tradeoffs

Making a decision about the best solution nearly always involves making a tradeoff. In the case of the best container for carrying soup, the plastic container with the screw-on lid was the best solution. But the plastic foam container is cheaper and does a good job of not leaking. So, you could choose it instead because it would be a more affordable option for you. A trade-off involves giving up something you like about one solution in order to get more of something else.

Risk-Benefit Analysis

Another tool engineers use to evaluate options is a risk-benefit analysis. A **risk-benefit analysis** compares the risks, or unfavorable effects of a solution, to the benefits, or favorable effects. A solution that has greater benefits and fewer risks is favored over one with fewer benefits and greater risks. For example, x-ray machines are tools that doctors use to see inside the body to evaluate and diagnose health problems. However, as x-rays pass through the body, they can damage living cells. Medical x-rays expose patients to very small doses of radiation. The risk of harm to cells is considered much smaller than the benefit of being able to diagnose health problems.

Select Promising Solutions

8. You have drawn a decision matrix to help assess how well several solutions meet the criteria of the problem "what type of chair is best to bring to the beach?" Four criteria and four solutions are written into the decision matrix. Your next step is to rank the importance of each criterion for a successful solution. Then fill out the matrix by awarding points to each solution based on how well they meet each criterion.

Criteria	Criterion rating (1–5)	Solutions			
		Folding camp chair	Inflatable beach float	Beach towel	Metal patio chair
Not expensive					
Easy to carry					
Washable					
Waterproof materials					
Totals					

What solution was the "best"? What type of trade-off would you need to make if you were to choose the second-highest scoring solution? Explain your answers.

_____

_____

_____

_____

_____

_____

Evaluating Solutions

A decision matrix helps you evaluate possible solutions. However, it does not provide every answer to address a design problem. The top-rated proposed solution to taking soup to school for lunch is the plastic container with the screw-on lid. This may well be the best way to carry soup to school. However, there are additional things you need to do before deciding this is the best solution. Solutions that seem to be perfectly workable sometimes do not actually solve the problem. After a solution or several possible solutions to a problem are identified, they are tested to identify whether they meet all the criteria and constraints of the problem. Testing several types of screw-top plastic containers that hold different volumes or have different styles of screw-top lids will help identify the best solution to your problem.

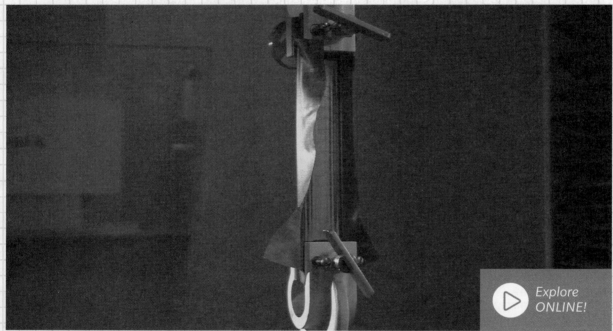

Explore ONLINE!

In some situations, machines such as this universal tester are used to test possible solutions. Many solutions do not perform exactly as expected in tests. Testing helps identify characteristics of a solution that work and those that do not.

9. An automotive engineering team proposes a new windshield coating that is designed to cause water to flow away from the windshield without using a wiper. Several different coatings have been recommended. Why is it important for the team to test all of the proposals before manufacturing the new windshields? Choose all answers that apply.

   A. Testing can determine whether one option is better than the others.

   B. Testing will confirm whether the coatings actually work in real situations.

   C. Testing may discover ways in which the coating performs better or worse than predicted.

   D. Testing may provide information on ways to improve the performance of the coatings.

Test Solutions

Similar to scientists, engineers rely on reproducible data in order to make and defend conclusions. Analyzing test results helps identify which solution is best and whether the best solution solves the problem. In order to be useful, a test measures one variable at a time. This provides information to evaluate the proposed solution and often leads to improvements in the design.

Some tests can be carried out using the solution exactly as proposed. For example, you can test which container best holds soup by testing the containers themselves. Sometimes, however, the actual solution cannot be tested directly. For example, engineers designing a large suspension bridge cannot build the bridge and then test it to see whether the design was right. Instead, they test a model of the bridge. A test model is called a **prototype.** Engineers use a prototype during the design process to test the design and make improvements. A prototype can be a physical, conceptual, mathematical, or computer-generated model.

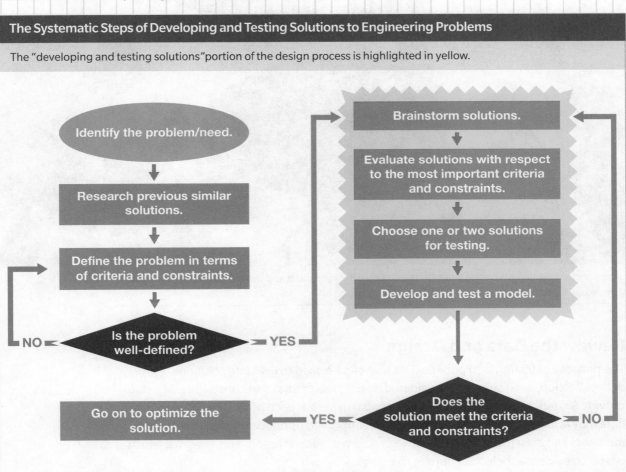

The Systematic Steps of Developing and Testing Solutions to Engineering Problems

The "developing and testing solutions" portion of the design process is highlighted in yellow.

Identify the problem/need.

Research previous similar solutions.

Define the problem in terms of criteria and constraints.

Is the problem well-defined? NO YES

Brainstorm solutions.

Evaluate solutions with respect to the most important criteria and constraints.

Choose one or two solutions for testing.

Develop and test a model.

Does the solution meet the criteria and constraints? NO YES

Go on to optimize the solution.

10. Each proposed solution is treated the same way in the engineering design process. Why is it important that every solution to a problem be tested the same way?

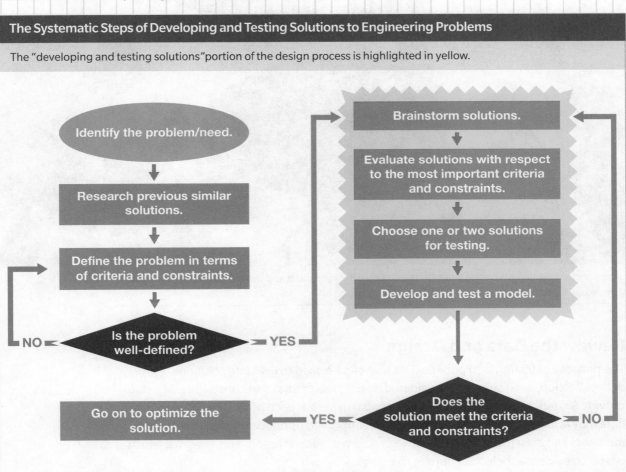

Evaluate Test Data

Engineers analyze test data to compare solutions and to determine how well each solution solves the problem. Many tests provide numerical data that can be compared mathematically. Every aspect of a solution can be tested, including the cost of materials and the time needed to implement the solution. These students are testing a parachute design model to see how long it takes to drop from the balcony. They want to develop a parachute that takes the longest time possible to drop. They will compare data from several tests and different designs to identify the best solution.

An important part of evaluating a design is building a design model and testing the model to measure the design's performance against criteria and constraints.

Review the Data and Design

The purpose of testing is to provide data that can be used to evaluate solutions. After data collection, each solution is evaluated against the criteria and constraints. The data provide evidence about the strengths and weaknesses of each proposed solution. The data may also indicate ways a solution can be improved upon. Using the data, team members can then provide constructive criticism of each solution. This analysis, which is based on evidence, helps to improve solutions.

11. Sometimes parts of different solutions can be combined to make a better solution. What benefit does this offer? Choose all that apply.

   A. It allows for the best part of each solution to be used in a final design.

   B. It gives the design team time to redefine the problem.

   C. It allows the designers to meet customer demands for new designs every year.

   D. It allows a solution to be developed that is better than earlier solutions.

   E. It allows each test variable to be tested fully in each test model.

Do the Math
Evaluate Parachute Designs

A group of students is designing a parachute system to drop an egg from a height of 3 meters without breaking the egg. The purpose of the first test was to compare the effectiveness of different parachute materials and sizes. To avoid making a mess, they tested their designs using a wooden block with a mass similar to that of an egg.

The variables in the tests were the parachute material and the parachute size. All of the test designs were dropped from the same point on the balcony using the same mass. The table below shows the averaged results after testing each design three times. Students then evaluated the data to determine which solution would most likely keep an egg from breaking.

Type of Parachute Material	Area of Parachute (cm²)	Time to Reach the Floor (s)
Cloth	500	1.7
Cloth	1000	2.2
Plastic film	500	2.7
Plastic film	1000	3.5
Paper	500	2.0
Paper	1000	2.5

12. Based on the evidence from the tests, make a recommendation about the type of material the students should use for their parachute. Explain your reasoning.

EVIDENCE NOTEBOOK

13. Why would a test that provides numerical data for each proposed solution for rescuing the kite from the tree be more useful than tests that do not provide numerical data? Record your evidence.

Hands-On Lab
Design a Model Car, Part 2

You will design and build a model car over several sessions. In the first step you defined the engineering problem by identifying the criteria and constraints of the problem. Next, you will propose design solutions to develop. Then you will evaluate the proposed solutions against the criteria.

Your challenge is to build the a model car using the supplied materials and specifications. Refer to the criteria, constraints and materials listed in Part 1 of this Hands-On Lab, which is in Lesson 1.

MATERIALS
• See materials from Design a Model Car, Part 1

Procedure

STEP 1 Brainstorm with your group to come up with several car designs to meet the challenge. Remember that your brainstorming ideas need to meet **all** the constraints to be valid.

STEP 2 Identify three design options that you want to explore further. Analyze how well these three design options meet the criteria of the problem using a decision matrix. The three criteria are listed in the matrix.

STEP 3 On a separate piece of paper, rank the importance of each criterion for the solution to be acceptable using a scale of 1 to 5 for each criterion, with 1 meaning "least important" and 5 meaning "most important." Then score each solution based on how well it meets each ranked criterion. Remember that points are awarded for each criterion up to but no more than the maximum value given to that criterion.

Criteria	Criterion rating (1–5)	Solutions		
		Car design 1	Car design 2	Car design 3
Travels the farthest				
Looks attractive				
Is reusable				
Totals				

STEP 4 **Draw** Based on your decision matrix, choose the design solution that scores the highest. This is the design that best meets the criteria. Draw a sketch of the design on a separate sheet of paper. Then, build your chosen design! Remember, you may use only the materials supplied by your teacher to build the car.

STEP 5 Any complex design project involves carrying out a number of tests to see how variables affect the performance of the design. There are several design variables that may affect the performance of the car. Some of these variables include the shape of the car, the weight of the car, and the location of the weights (washers) on the body.

Choose one variable to test to identify how it affects the distance traveled by the car. Remember to check the race specifications to be sure you are testing only values that are within the allowed range for your car.

STEP 6 Design a test to evaluate the effect of the one variable on the distance the car travels. Explain how the test will be carried out.

STEP 7 Using a test ramp, conduct the test. Record your results on a separate sheet of paper.

STEP 8 You may, if time allows, identify and test another variable to see how it affects your car's performance.

Analysis

STEP 9 On a separate sheet of paper, draw a graph showing the relationship of the change in your variable to the distance the car traveled. Draw a graph for each variable tested. Evaluate the effect of the variable on the distance traveled. State a conclusion about the effect the variable had on the distance the car traveled.

STEP 10 One member of your group suggests that to save time, two variables that may affect the distance traveled can be tested at the same time. Is this an acceptable way to test a design solution? Explain your answer.

STEP 11 Ideally, several tests that investigate the effect of different variables on the performance of the design solution are carried out. What is the purpose of carrying out so many tests on a design solution?

Engage in Argument from Evidence

Critical analysis of solutions includes using data to make suggestions for improvement to the solution. A conclusion that is not supported by data is not useful to the design process.

14. After deciding to use a plastic film parachute to slow the fall of an egg, students tested different parachute sizes and again tested them by dropping a parachute and mass from a height of 3 m. Each parachute was tested three times. The average time to reach the floor is recorded on the table.

Area of Parachute (cm²)	Time to Reach the Floor (s)
100	1.0
250	1.5
500	2.2
1000	3.0
1500	2.7
2000	2.1

One student argued that a parachute with a larger area is always better because it provides more air resistance. Explain how the data supports or does not support that argument.

_____

_____

_____

_____

_____

15. What size parachute would be the most suited to slow the fall of an egg? Use data from the table to support your conclusion.

_____

_____

_____

_____

_____

16. Why is systematic testing of possible solutions needed before choosing a design to refine and optimize?

_____

_____

_____

_____

_____

Continue Your Exploration

Name: _____ Date: _____

Check out the path below or go online to choose one of the other paths shown.

| Building on Earlier Solutions | • Hands-On Labs 🖐
• Using Data to Make Informed Decisions
• Propose Your Own Path | Go online to choose one of these other paths. |

The incandescent light bulb is a common technology. Thomas Edison is often thought of as its inventor, but he did not invent it. However, in 1878, he and his team developed the first practical and commercially successful incandescent bulb. Edison approached the design of the light bulb as an engineering problem. He needed to develop a bulb that would produce enough light but not burn out quickly. He and his assistants tested thousands of materials and setups. In fact, Edison stated, "I have not failed. I've just found 10,000 ways that won't work."

Many Solutions Tested

Some of Edison's designs used a filament. A bulb filament is the part that lights up. It is a thin wire through which electric current flows. Some of the filament designs did not work because the material did not carry enough electric current. Others worked for a short period and then burned out. By combining what Edison and his team had learned in many tests, they eventually found a solution—a metal filament in a vacuum tube.

Edison's success in making a light bulb included using data collected from numerous experiments to help brainstorm new ideas. His team tested many different materials and configurations to find a workable solution. Brainstorming was part of the process, although Edison and his team would not have used that term. By remaining open to many possible solutions and knowing that "failure" was an important part of the learning process, Edison eventually solved the problem.

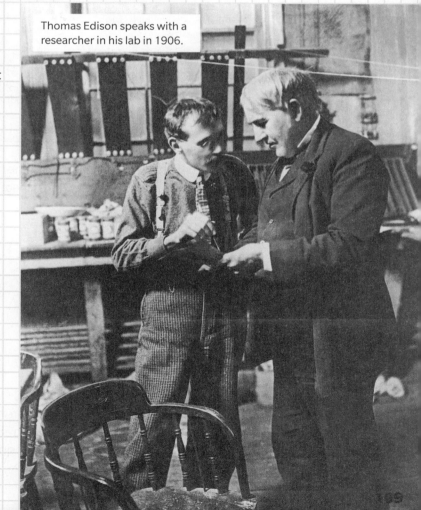

Thomas Edison speaks with a researcher in his lab in 1906.

169

Continue Your Exploration

1. How would the usefulness of the incandescent bulb have been affected if electrical supply systems were not developed?

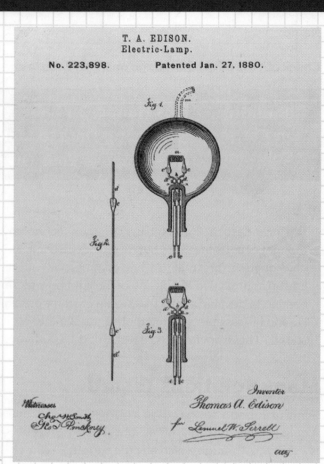

T. A. EDISON.
Electric-Lamp.

No. 223,898.   Patented Jan. 27, 1880.

Fig. 1

Fig. 2

Fig. 3

Witnesses
Chas H Smith
Geo. T. Pinckney.

Inventor
Thomas A. Edison

for Lemuel W. Serrell

2. Explain how Edison and his team used test evidence to determine whether they had reached a solution to the problem. How did that evidence determine whether they should continue to develop the solution?

This is Edison's patent filing for his light bulb design. A patent is a license from the government that legally protects an invention from being copied or sold by others.

3. The term *brainstorming* was not used in Edison's time but the descriptions of his research imply that his team used the technique. What aspect of Edison's research supports this idea?

4. **Collaborate** Work with your group to research the solution to an engineering problem that has had an impact on society. Find out who developed the first workable solution and how ideas were tested during the design process.

Can You Explain It?

Name: _____ **Date:** _____

Review the problem of getting your kite out of a tree.

How would you develop and test ways to get your kite out of a tree?

EVIDENCE NOTEBOOK

Refer to the notes in your Evidence Notebook to help you propose several solutions to the problem of retrieving the kite from the tree.

1. State your claim. Make sure your claim fully explains how to develop and test a solution to solve the problem.

2. Explain evidence that supports the process of developing and testing solutions. How does your evidence connect to and support your claim?

Checkpoints

Answer the following questions to check your understanding of the lesson.

Use the photograph to answer Question 3.

3. How does prioritizing criteria help designers develop a better helmet? Choose all that apply.

A. It automatically ranks constraints too because they are the same as criteria.

B. It identifies the most important criteria that a solution must meet.

C. It helps in assessing several solutions that meet the criteria of the problem.

D. It helps to eliminate solutions that do not meet the constraints.

Use the photograph to answer Question 4.

4. Technical drawings require a writing tool that can make very precise and fine marks. Identify things you would do to help identify the best technical drawing pen from several different types of pens. Choose all that apply.

A. Identify whether each pen meets the criteria of your technical drawing problem.

B. Identify pens that do not meet the constraints of your technical drawing problem.

C. Test the pens to see which one best meets the criteria.

D. Rank the criteria of the problem in their order of importance for a successful solution.

5. Why is using models an important part of the testing process? Choose all that apply.

A. They allow designers to brainstorm better ideas.

B. They allow the design solution to be tested when the actual solution itself cannot be tested.

C. They allow design solutions to be tested in a systematic way.

D. Their use provides engineers with lots of data to evaluate the performance of a possible design solution.

6. A team of students is designing a robot to compete in a race. They select three ideas to develop further. Which statements describe the steps the team might take to identify the best robot design? Choose all that apply.

A. Build and test models of each design.

B. Choose a team leader who will choose the design to build.

C. Evaluate test data for each design and see how each one meets the criteria and constraints of the problem.

D. Use the design that looks the best and discard the others.

Interactive Review

Complete this interactive study guide to review the lesson.

Engineering solutions are developed by proposing ideas and then comparing how well those ideas meet the criteria and constraints of the problem.

A. How is a decision matrix useful during the development of a solution to an engineering design problem?

Testing provides data that can be used to rank proposed solutions and evaluate the effects of changes to design solutions.

B. Why is analyzing data from tests important to improving a design solution?

Optimizing Solutions

The Akashi Kaikyo Bridge spans 3.9 km (2.43 miles) across the Akashi Strait. It links the city of Kobe with Awaji-shima Island in Japan. It is the longest suspension bridge in the world.

By the end of this lesson . . .

you will be able to design and perform tests and analyze the results in order to optimize a design solution.

CAN YOU EXPLAIN IT?

What is the best way to keep plates from breaking on hard floors?

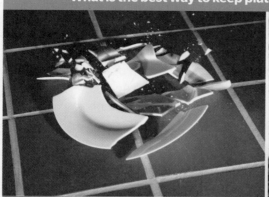 

Most kitchens have hard floors, which are easy to clean. However, if a plate is dropped on a hard surface, it will break. Several solutions to prevent breaking plates are available. Identifying the solution that works the best and making it better is called optimization.

1. Imagine you are a chef in a busy kitchen. You need to reduce the number of plates that break because broken plates are a safety hazard and they need to be replaced. What are five potential solutions to this problem?

2. Optimizing a solution involves a process of testing a design solution in order to refine it and make it the best it can be to solve a problem. Choose the solution you think is most appropriate for the problem above. Identify ways you could test it in order to make it the best solution for your problem.

 EVIDENCE NOTEBOOK As you explore this lesson, gather information to help explain how the best solution to a problem is determined.

Improving a Promising Design Solution

Treats, such as muffins, are designed to taste delicious. Some muffin recipes make large and fluffy muffins. Other recipes make smaller, denser muffins. Each recipe uses different amounts of ingredients, such as baking powder, that make them light or dense. Imagine that you found a recipe for blueberry muffins that is rated as "delicious" by reviewers. You want to make the muffins for a party. Your design problem is to create muffins that are bite-sized and do not crumble. So you want to test the recipe first. If the muffins are too dense, people might not like them. If they are too fluffy, they will likely break apart when people bite into them. You follow the recipe. Then you test your design by tasting a muffin. It falls apart. It is too crumbly. It needs to be denser.

Build on the Most Promising Design

You have a design solution (a recipe), but it is currently not the best solution to your problem (to make small muffins for the party). You need to experiment to optimize the recipe. You will make several batches of muffins and change the amount of baking powder in each batch. The only way to know what such changes might do is to test the recipes and check the results!

Design optimization is the process of making an object or system as effective and useful as possible. A design solution, whether it is a blueberry muffin recipe or an engine part, is always tested to determine whether it is a better solution than any of those previously tested. Improvements to a design are made in response to test results.

Testing the recipe and modifying it based on your results will lead to a recipe that best meets your needs.

3. Optimizing a design solution always involves testing the modified solution. Why is it helpful to replicate these tests? Use the example of the muffin recipe in your answer.

Make Trade-offs

Analysis of test data gives information about how a solution will perform in real-life situations. Data analysis also helps determine whether a design solution can be built within a given budget or whether it can meet constraints on the retail cost. These types of analyses do not always provide definite answers as to which solution is best. Sometimes trade-offs are necessary to come to the solution that is most likely to meet the needed criteria. For example, a metal case for a cell phone might increase the lifetime of the phone. However, a plastic case is much less expensive and is lighter in weight, which customers prefer. The designer might therefore choose to go with a plastic case. A trade-off is made between a longer lifetime for the product and a lower cost and a lighter weight. Identifying which criteria are most important, such as "lower cost" and "lighter weight" instead of "a longer lifetime," are necessary to move to the next steps in the optimization process.

4. Why is making a trade-off an important part of optimizing a design? Choose all that apply.

   A. It helps to identify more criteria.

   B. It gets rid of unnecessary constraints.

   C. It helps identify what the designer needs to do next.

   D. It helps identify the most important features the design solution should have.

Test Models

In selecting the best solution, engineers often perform tests on a type of model called a prototype. A **prototype** is a test model of a design solution. Prototypes are usually the first model of a new design. They are built for testing and may be shown to others to get feedback for improving the design. A prototype may be a physical, mathematical, or computer model. Sometimes a physical model is an actual working example of the design, but often, especially for large or complex designs, it may be a scale model of the object or even just a part of the object. Prototypes can also be tested for design flaws, safety, and ease of use. These tests help ensure that everything works the way it should and that customers can figure out how to make it work. Otherwise, the product may become an expensive design failure.

Engineers use prototypes to identify precise changes to the design. This shoe prototype was printed using a 3D printer.

Evaluate Advantages and Disadvantages

After testing, solutions can be further evaluated using tools such as a cost-benefit analysis. A *cost-benefit analysis* is a method of identifying the strengths and weaknesses of a design solution. One example is comparing the production costs to the benefits the solution offers. A cost-benefit analysis helps determine which solutions are most promising. This kind of analysis can be used to develop and refine solutions at several points throughout the design process.

Do the Math
Use Math for Design Improvement

In order to minimize costs for the manufacturer, processed food is often packaged in containers that allow the maximum storage volume but use the minimal amount of materials. The best design solution for a cereal box can be chosen by calculating the box dimensions that best meet the criteria of a maximum volume while using the least amount of cardboard.

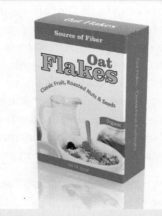

Containers with a large surface area allow the manufacturer to better advertise their product.

The table below shows some calculations that engineers made while creating a cereal box. Your task is to find the cereal box size that has the maximum volume and the least surface area, or the least amount of cardboard used to make the box. The design constraints that have been set are as follows:

The volume must be between 3400 cm^3 and 3425 cm^3.
The height must be between 25 and 27 cm.
The length must be between 18 and 20 cm.
The width must be between 6 and 8 cm.

Height (cm)	Length (cm)	Width (cm)	Volume (cm^3)	Surface Area (SA) (cm^2)	Volume to SA (ratio)
25.5	20.0	6.6	3417	1630	
27.0	19.0	6.7	3437	1642	
26.5	19.0	6.8	3424	1626	
26.0	19.0	6.9	3409	1609	
25.5	19.0	7.0	3392	1592	
27.0	18.0	7.1	3451	1611	
26.5	18.0	7.2	3434	1595	
26.0	18.0	7.3	3416	1578	
25.5	18.0	7.4	3397	1562	

5. For each set of box dimensions, determine the volume to surface area ratio. Round the results to two decimal places. Choose the box that best meets the constraints and explain your reasoning.

6. Why do design engineers further test the most promising solution to a problem such as preventing plates from breaking, before finalizing the design? Record your evidence.

Identify the Characteristics of the Best Solution

One design may not perform the best across all tests, so identifying the characteristics of the design that performed best in each test can help design the best solution to the problem. This is an important step in optimizing the solution for any engineering problem.

Optimizing a raincoat design involves working with a design that combines the most favorable characteristics.

A raincoat designer wants to make raincoats that teenagers would like. The company's engineers tested three different designs that performed well in three different tests. However, no design performed the best in all the tests. The design criteria is identified as follows:

• It must be as lightweight as possible.
• It must to be easy to close and open.
• It must be as water resistant as possible.
• It must be made of fabrics with fashionable designs and colors.
• It must have pockets.

	Weight (grams)	Closure	Fabric (minutes in water until it leaks)
Raincoat A	250	Snaps: hard to use	11
Raincoat B	410	Zipper: easy to use	27
Raincoat C	500	Zipper: easy to use	>60

The three criteria identified as the most important for a successful design were: being lightweight, being easy to close, and having high water resistance. Engineers chose to test a design that combined the best features of each raincoat. The redesign had the weight range of Raincoat A, the water resistant fabric of Raincoat C, and the zipper of Raincoats B and C. The redesigned raincoat was then tested. Tests showed that the most water resistant fabric worked in the new lightweight design.

7. Imagine you are in charge of further optimizing the raincoat design. What would be the next steps you would take in the optimization process?

Using Data to Optimize Solutions

Some engineering problems involve designing a process or system rather than designing an object. The assembly line is an example of a system that has become an important manufacturing system. In an automotive assembly line, a car's frame moves on an automated belt system. As the cars or their parts move by, each worker along the line performs a specific task. At the end of the assembly line, there is a finished car. The assembly line is an engineering process designed to solve an engineering problem— making many similar or identical objects as efficiently as possible. Assembly lines are used to produce many things, such as clothing, tools, food, and vehicles.

Process and System Optimization

Engineered systems are designed to solve a well-defined problem. Although assembly line systems were used during the Industrial Revolution to speed up the manufacturing process, they were not optimized until the early 20th century to include the types of processes that are used today.

Henry Ford and his team designed the first modern assembly line to produce large numbers of cars. Each major car part was produced on a separate line. Then a final line assembled the vehicle. Every worker carried out a specific task. The time needed to build a single car dropped from 12 hours to about 90 minutes. Optimizing assembly lines allowed Ford's main factory to increase production from fewer than 20,000 cars a year to more than a million cars per year in just 10 years. Ford was able to reduce the price of his cars by reducing the time, cost, and number of people it took to build them.

The assembly line has changed through continual optimization. Today, assembly lines are often made up of rows of robots doing repetitive tasks for long periods of time instead of rows of human workers doing the same thing.

8. The assembly line has changed over time. How is the optimization of engineering processes similar to the optimization of engineering products?

The Iterative Design Process

Part of design optimization includes iterative testing of a prototype. The results of iterative tests are used to improve the next design version. For example, a company that makes bicycle parts is designing a new gear sprocket. Bicycle sprockets are most often made from an alloy of aluminum and zinc. The alloy is light and is available in a variety of strengths. The sprocket design works well, but designers now want to make it from the strongest alloy they can. To identify the most suitable alloy, designers will test the sprocket design using different alloys. Strength tests will identify the strongest alloy. The sprocket design will be modified to use the new, stronger alloy.

Several sprockets make up the gears of a bicycle.

The Systematic Steps of Optimizing a Design Solution

Iterative design processes are used to optimize the solution. The optimizing steps are highlighted.

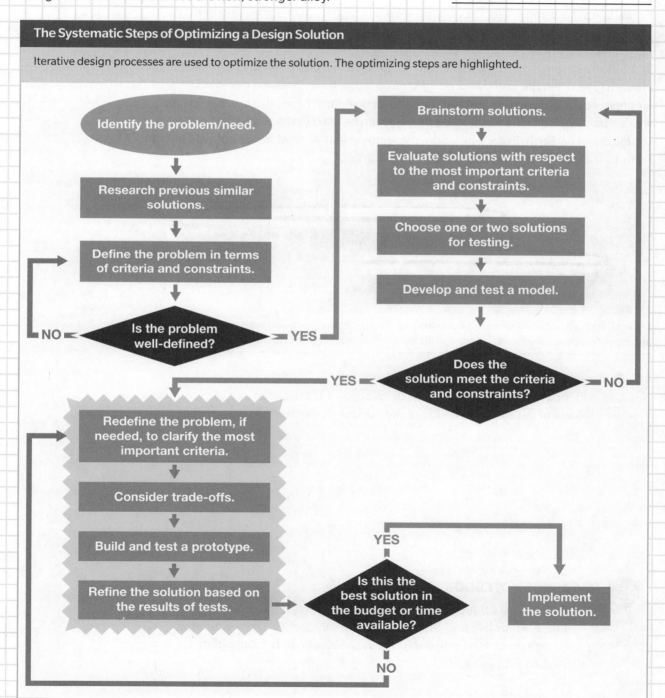

9. What are some characteristics of the iterative design process? Choose all that apply.

    A. Each iteration incorporates features that worked in previous tests.

    B. Useful features of different solutions can be combined.

    C. Solutions are tested during every iteration of the design process.

    D. Each iteration starts with a completely new idea or solution.

The Space Pen

An example of a product of the iterative design process is the "space pen," a ballpoint pen that can work in zero gravity. Astronauts on early space missions used pencils to keep notes, but using pencils created problems. Broken tips and graphite dust floated around the cabin and interfered with instruments. The developer of the space pen, Paul Fisher, used the iterative process to optimize the design solution for writing in space. In the freefall conditions of space, the ink in a regular pen dried out, or it did not flow in the right direction. Fisher designed a cartridge to hold the ink. However, a vacuum formed in the cartridge and the ink stopped flowing. To solve this problem, he pressurized the ink cartridge. Then the ink flowed well. However, sometimes it leaked because of the air pressure. To improve the performance, Fisher developed a gel-like ink that flowed well and did not leak. The result was a pen that can be used in space and that can write upside down on Earth. In each iteration, the features that worked were improved and the features that did not work were not developed further.

During the iterative design process used to develop the space pen, many solutions were tested. Each iteration of proposed solutions and test results led to more improvements in the pen's design.

10. Sometimes the solution for one problem leads to new solutions to other problems. Use evidence from the example of the development of the space pen to explain how the problem of developing a ballpoint pen for use on Earth was likely redefined.

 EVIDENCE NOTEBOOK

    11. Even after a solution is implemented, engineers often return to the original problem and work to refine the solution. How is the iterative design process helpful is developing a solution to breaking plates? Record your evidence.

Hands-On Lab
Design a Model Car: Part 3

Now that you have built your model car, you and other groups in your class will evaluate test data and optimize the design of your cars. The exact steps of your optimization process can vary depending on the number of cars built, the time available, and how your class is divided into groups.

Refer to the instructions in Part 1 of this lab for the criteria and constraints for the car designs and the materials list.

MATERIALS
• See materials from Design a Model Car, Part 1.

Procedure and Analysis

STEP 1 Compare the test results of your car from Part 2 of this lab with the results of other groups who tested the same car design variables. Describe how those variables are related to the distance traveled.

STEP 2 Are there characteristics of other groups' cars that performed better in the tests than your car? Based on your comparison of the class results, propose three design changes that could improve your car's performance. List your proposed design changes. Identify how you think the proposed design change will improve the car's performance.

STEP 3 With your teacher's approval, apply one design change to your car. Repeat the test and record your data on a separate sheet of paper. Compare the data from your modified design to the data from your original design.

STEP 4 How did the design change affect performance?

STEP 5 As a class, evaluate all of the test results and make suggestions for a new iteration of the design, using the best characteristics of each design.

© Houghton Mifflin Harcourt

STEP 6 Each component of the solution must relate to the problem as it is defined. For example, unless the clearance the car body must have from the ground meets specifications for the ramp on which the cars will roll down, the car might get stuck as it leaves the ramp. How do the car's wheels relate to the car as a solution to the engineering problem?

STEP 7 How does taking the best performing characteristics of different car designs and using them to redesign your car help improve it?

Combine the Best Parts of Solutions

After a product is introduced, the iterative process continues, often leading to development of new models or new styles. Each new style is a solution to a restated design problem that is influenced by successes and failures of the previous solutions. For example, cell phones have changed significantly over time, as shown here. Touchscreens have replaced keypads, and antennas are contained within the phone. Optimization of the phone's built-in camera has added a major new function to cell phones. Inexpensive point-and-shoot cameras, once popular devices, have been almost entirely replaced by cell phones.

During the optimization of cell phones, trade-offs were necessary.

12. Improvements of one function frequently lead to worse performance of another function. Which of these statements describe a trade-off that was needed as cell phones changed to meet new criteria and constraints? Choose all that apply.

   A. Larger cell phone screens allow new functions, such as viewing videos.

   B. Adding more applications shortens the life of a battery charge.

   C. Bigger screens increase the amount of glass surface, making it easier to shatter.

   D. Internal antennas increase portability but decrease signal reception.

   E. Touchscreens increase viewing area but are harder for some people to use than buttons.

   F. Thinner cases decrease the weight of the phone and make it easier to handle.

13. How might starting the engineering design process with only one idea affect the ability to optimize that design later on?

_____

_____

_____

Continue Your Exploration

Name: _____   Date: _____

Check out the path below or go online to choose one of the other paths shown.

People in Engineering

- **Hands-On Labs** ✋
- **Rapid Prototyping (3D Printers)**
- **Propose Your Own Path**

Go online to choose one of these other paths.

Ellen Ochoa, Electrical Engineer

Ellen Ochoa is an astronaut and the director of the Johnson Space Center in Houston, Texas. As a student working on her doctorate in electrical engineering, and later as a researcher at NASA, she designed optical data systems for processing information using light signals. She became an astronaut in 1991, and flew on four Space Shuttle missions. Her jobs included developing software and computer hardware for space flights, and robotics development and testing. Besides being an astronaut, a manager, and a research engineer, Ochoa is a classical flutist. She lives in Texas with her husband and their two children.

Electrical engineers design, develop, and test electrical equipment, such as electric motors, radar and navigation systems, communications systems, and power generation equipment. They also supervise the manufacturing of this equipment. Electrical engineers who work in industrial careers often have bachelor's degrees. Electrical engineers who direct research at university and government labs frequently have a doctorate. As Ellen Ochoa has shown, the sky is not the limit for electrical engineers.

Dr. Ochoa became the first Hispanic woman to go to space when she served as a mission specialist aboard the space shuttle Discovery in 1993.

Continue Your Exploration

1. List three industries that would likely employ electrical engineers. Then describe one job that would likely involve electrical engineering in each industry.

2. Why might a person who is thinking about studying electrical engineering need to think about whether they enjoy solving problems?

3. Ellen Ochoa was accepted by NASA as an astronaut after she became an electrical engineer and established her career as one. Why would a career in electrical engineering be useful as an astronaut?

4. **Collaborate** Research one or more electrical engineers who are involved in research. On a sheet of paper, generate a list of questions to ask the engineers about their work. With your teacher's help, contact one or more of these engineers to interview. Present your findings to the class.

Can You Explain It?

Name: _____   Date: _____

Examine the photos as you revisit the problem of breaking plates.

What is the best way to keep plates from breaking on hard floors?

 EVIDENCE NOTEBOOK

Refer to the notes in your Evidence Notebook to help you decide how to optimize the solution to the stated engineering problem.

1. State your claim. Make sure your reasoning fully explains how a solution may be optimized to solve the problem.

2. Explain the importance of optimizing a solution. How does the evidence you gathered connect to and support your claim?

Checkpoints

Answer the following questions to check your understanding of the lesson.
Use the data in the table to answer Questions 3–5.

3. Your team is building a rocket to enter into a national competition. Scoring is based on three factors: how high the rocket flies, time of flight before the parachute opens, and how well it safely delivers a cargo of three eggs. These criteria are of equal importance to your design. You test four different design solutions and record the results, which are averaged here.

	Height (meters)	Time of flight (seconds)	Number of eggs unbroken
Rocket A	260	49	3
Rocket B	220	57	1
Rocket C	240	66	3
Rocket D	275	58	2

Evaluate the test results to decide which design is the best for you to optimize.

A. Rocket A
B. Rocket B
C. Rocket C
D. Rocket D

4. The iterative process involves testing the most promising solutions and modifying the design based on test results. Is there a feature of a different rocket design that you would like to include in the design you chose in Question 3? If so, explain your reasoning.

5. Your tests show that the key detail for high flight is the ratio of length to diameter. You want to improve the height your rocket design can reach. Which of the following should you incorporate into the new design? Choose all that apply.

A. the dimensions of Rocket A
B. the dimensions of Rocket B
C. the dimensions of Rocket C
D. the dimensions of Rocket D

This engineer is testing the strength of different structural designs for use in the construction of a bridge.

Use the photograph to answer Question 6.

6. What are some advantages of using scale model prototypes before building actual bridge pillars? Choose all that apply.

A. Scale models are less expensive to construct than actual pillars.

B. Using models allows the engineer to test many different combinations of materials.

C. The engineer will be able to find the best combination of materials for the bridge.

D. Models are able to exactly reproduce the function of a pillar, but the testing is faster.

Interactive Review

Complete this interactive study guide to review the lesson.

The solution that best addresses the ranked criteria of the engineering problem, and performs best in tests, is chosen to further refine.

A. Why is it important to compare test results when making decisions about what design to develop further?

The iterative design process is a tool that engineers use to build the best solution. It is used to identify ways a solution can be improved further to better address the criteria and constraints of the design problem.

B. After a solution has been built, why might engineers want to optimize it further? What design process would they likely use to optimize a solution?

Choose one of the activities below to explore how this unit connects to other topics.

Social Studies Connection

Epic Failures Many inventors and scientists "failed" before making a big discovery. The Wright Brothers became successful only after experimenting with hundreds of glider flights and airplane designs.

Research and make a verbal presentation about another person in history who persevered through adversity before having his or her invention succeed. Describe how the inventor refined the device using the engineering design process.

Art Connection

Scientific Illustrations Artists often engage in a version of the engineering design process when trying a new technique or approach. Artists start with reference materials to create technical illustrations. They engage in multiple trials with techniques and mediums to determine the best process for the artwork. Based on feedback, they repeat this process to refine the final design.

Research various technical drawings to examine how the scientific steps are illustrated. Then create your own visual representation or diagram showing how an everyday object works. Seek feedback from a classmate and make modifications based on his or her understanding of your design.

Life Science Connection

Biomedicine Medical biology, or biomedicine, is the application of biological research to medical practices. This field of study includes specialties ranging from laboratory diagnostics to vaccine development and gene therapy. Engineers in the field of biomedicine work to design biomedical devices and develop biotechnologies.

Research a biomedical invention, therapy, or process and the history of its development. Prepare a multimedia presentation describing how the engineering design process contributed to the evolution of a successful treatment solution.

Name: _____ Date: _____

Complete this review to check your understanding of the unit.

Use the diagram to answer Questions 1–3.

1. At which step in the engineering design process would a decision matrix be useful for narrowing the proposed solutions for further testing and analysis?

   A. brainstorm solutions

   B. evaluate solutions with respect to criteria

   C. develop and test a model

   D. evaluate test data

2. At which step in the engineering design process can constructive evidence-based criticism be used to analyze the success of a proposed solution?

   A. brainstorm solutions

   B. evaluate solutions with respect to criteria

   C. choose solutions for testing

   D. evaluate test data

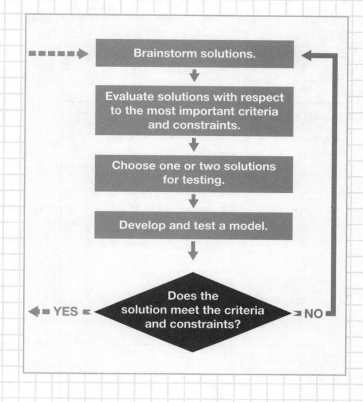

3. Testing and evaluating solutions is a(n) _iterative / linear_ process.

Use the decision matrix to answer Questions 4–5.

Decision Matrix: The best screen protector			
Criteria	**Materials**		
	TPU	Tempered Glass	PET Film
Does not scratch	2	4	4
Reduces glare	2	3	2
Lightweight	2	2	1
Durable	1	4	4
Not Expensive	3	1	2

4. This decision matrix ranks screen protector materials according to several specifications. Which material would make the best screen protector if the most important features were *Not Expensive* and *Reduces glare*?

   A. TPU (thermoplastic polyurethane)

   B. Tempered Glass

   C. PET Film (polyethylene terephthalate)

5. The screen protector materials are the _criteria / solutions_ in the decision matrix. The specifications about each option are the _criteria / solutions_.

Name: _____   **Date:** _____

6. Think about the engineering design process as you fill out this chart. Describe how each of the steps involves aspects of each of the big picture concepts.

Process Steps	Criteria and Constraints	Research and Data Analysis	Systems and System Models
Defining an engineering problem	Determining the most important criteria and constraints helps to precisely define the design problem by identifying specific needs and limitations.		
Testing a solution			
Making trade-offs			

Use the photograph of the mind-controlled prosthetic arm to answer Questions 7–10.

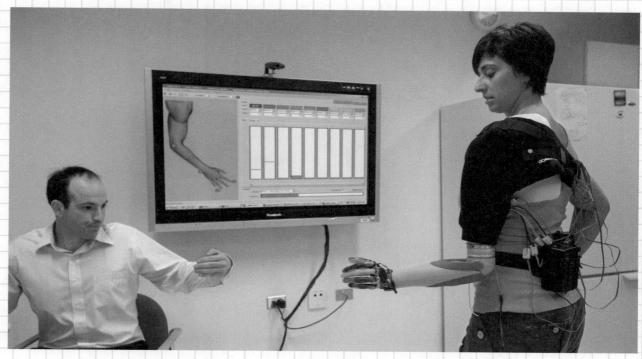

7. The photo shows a woman controlling the movements of her prosthetic arm using brain signals. Describe the problem that this tool solves.

8. People using this new type of prosthetic have noticed that some of their needs are not met by the current design. Based on these comments, the engineers are working to address these issues and are developing a new prototype. Explain why a new prototype is necessary.

9. What criteria do you think the inventors determined were important when developing their prototype?

10. Describe how this invention illustrates the practices of engineering.

Use the photographs to answer Questions 11–14.

11. Precisely state the problems that each of these suitcases solve. Are they the same problems? Explain your answer.

12. What kinds of data could you collect about suitcase designs? What tests would be the most helpful in comparing how each solution solves the design problem?

13. After analyzing the data about suitcase designs, you may find that both options have good features. Explain how engineers might use these results to develop an improved solution.

14. Suitcase designs have changed over time. Use evidence to explain why suitcases have benefited from the engineering design process.

Name: _____   Date: _____

What is the best feature for a new pool entry ramp?

An inspector has determined that the entrance ramp for your community pool does not meet current safety requirements. The pool management board is looking at ways to change the current design to better meet safety standards. They are looking at changing the ramp angle, surface material, and/or the railings.

Your team has been asked to analyze design solutions to determine which ramp is the best choice for your community pool. You will present your findings to the community pool directors as they decide how to proceed.

The steps below will help guide your research and develop your recommendation.

Engineer It

1. **Define the Problem** Clearly identify the criteria and constraints associated with the redesign of the pool ramp. How could each type of modification increase ramp safety for different types of pool patrons?

Engineer It

2. **Conduct Research** Consider each of the three pool ramp feature options. Explain what types of work would have to be done in order to make that type of ramp modification.

3. **Analyze Data** Create a decision matrix to analyze the modification options. Describe the strengths and weaknesses of each choice. How well does each change increase safety for the patrons of the pool?

4. **Identify and Recommend a Solution** Based on your research, construct a written explanation about which pool ramp feature is the best choice for your community pool. Describe any trade-offs involved in your decision.

5. **Communicate** Prepare a presentation of your recommendation for the community pool directors as they decide which design is best for the ramp. Include an argument for your recommendation based on evidence and an explanation of the benefits and drawbacks associated with the design.

✓ **Self-Check**

	I precisely defined the criteria and constraints associated with the problem of improving the safety of the pool ramp.
	I researched the design features to determine how well they meet the criteria and constraints of the problem.
	I analyzed my research and data to create a decision matrix.
	My solution is based on evidence from research, data, and an analysis of my decision matrix.
	My solution and recommendation was clearly communicated to others.

© Houghton Mifflin Harcourt

Glossary

\multicolumn{8}{c}{Pronunciation Key}

Sound	Symbol	Example	Respelling	Sound	Symbol	Example	Respelling
ă	a	pat	PAT	ŏ	ah	bottle	BAHT'l
ā	ay	pay	PAY	ō	oh	toe	TOH
âr	air	care	KAIR	ô	aw	caught	KAWT
ä	ah	father	FAH•ther	ôr	ohr	roar	ROHR
är	ar	argue	AR•gyoo	oi	oy	noisy	NOYZ•ee
ch	ch	chase	CHAYS	o͞o	u	book	BUK
ĕ	e	pet	PET	o͞o	oo	boot	BOOT
ĕ (at end of a syllable)	eh	settee lessee	seh•TEE leh•SEE	ou	ow	pound	POWND
ĕr	ehr	merry	MEHR•ee	s	s	center	SEN•ter
ē	ee	beach	BEECH	sh	sh	cache	CASH
g	g	gas	GAS	ŭ	uh	flood	FLUHD
ĭ	i	pit	PIT	ûr	er	bird	BERD
ĭ (at end of a syllable)	ih	guitar	gih•TAR	z	z	xylophone	ZY•luh•fohn
ī	y eye (only for a complete syllable)	pie island	PY EYE•luhnd	z	z	bags	BAGZ
îr	ir	hear	HIR	zh	zh	decision	dih•SIZH •uhn
j	j	germ	JERM	ə	uh	around broken focus	uh•ROWND BROH•kuhn FOH•kuhs
k	k	kick	KIK	ər	er	winner	WIN•er
ng	ng	thing	THING	th	th	thin they	THIN THAY
ngk	ngk	bank	BANGK	w	w	one	WUHN
				wh	hw	whether	HWETH•er

A–Z

boundary (BOWN•duh•ree)
a limit that defines the edges of a system and the divisions within a system (29)
frontera   límite que define los márgenes de un sistema y las divisiones que tiene dentro

brainstorming (BRAYN•stohr•ming)
the process of working alone or with others to quickly and freely generate ideas to solve a problem (99)
lluvia de ideas   proceso de trabajar individual o colectivamente para generar ideas de manera rápida y sin reservas con el objetivo de resolver un problema

component (kuhm•PO•nent)
the parts of a system that interact and carry out a process or processes (28)
componente   partes de un sistema que interactúan y llevan a cabo un proceso o varios procesos

constraints (kuhn•STRAYNTS)
limitations that define the boundaries of a design process (52, 85)
restricciones   limitaciones que definen las fronteras de un proceso de diseño

criteria (kry•TIR•ee•uh)
the specific requirements and standards a design must meet (52, 84)
criterios   requisitos y estándares específicos que un diseño debe cumplir

decision matrix (dih•SIZH•uhn MAY•triks)
a decision-making tool for evaluating several options at the same time (100)
matriz de decisiones   instrumento de toma de decisión que permite evaluar varias opciones a la vez

design optimization (dih•ZYN ahp•tuh•mih•ZAY•shun)
the process or method of making a design or system as fully functional or effective as possible (116)
optimización del diseño   proceso o método para lograr que un diseño o sistema sea completamente funcional o lo más eficaz posible

engineering (en•juh•NIR•ing)
the application of science and mathematics to solve real-life problems (6)
ingeniería   la aplicación de las ciencias y las matemáticas para resolver problemas de la vida diaria

input (IN•put)
information, material, or energy added to a system or process (28)
entrada   información, material o energía que ingresa a un sistema o proceso

iterative testing (IT•uh•ruh•tiv TEST•ing)
a type of design testing that is repeated many times as part of the engineering design process; the results of each repetition are used to modify the next version of the product or tool (55)
pruebas iterativas   tipo de prueba de diseño que se repite muchas veces como parte del proceso de diseño de ingeniería; los resultados de cada repetición se utilizan para modificar la próxima versión del producto o herramienta

output (OWT•put)
information, material, or energy resulting from a system or process (28)
salida   información, material o energía resultante de un sistema o proceso

prototype (PROH•tuh•typ)
a test model of a product (103)
prototipo   prueba modelo de un producto

risk-benefit analysis (risk•BEN•uh•fit uh•NAL•ih•sis)
the comparison of the risks and benefits of a decision or product (101)
análisis de riesgo-beneficio   la comparación de los riesgos y los beneficios de una decisión o de un producto

system (SIS•tuhm)
a set of interacting parts that work together; sometimes considered distinct from their surroundings only for the purpose of study (28)
sistema   conjunto de partes interconectadas que trabajan juntas; a veces se lo considera diferente o distinto de su entorno solo con el fin de cumplir los propósitos de una investigación

technology (tek•NAHL•uh•jee)
the application of science for practical purposes; the use of tools, machines, materials, and processes to meet human needs (6)
tecnología   la aplicación de la ciencia con fines prácticos; el uso de herramientas, máquinas, materiales y procesos para satisfacer las necesidades de los seres humanos

Index

Page numbers for key terms are in **boldface** type.
Page numbers in *italic* type indicate illustrative material, such as photographs, graphs, charts and maps.

© Houghton Mifflin Harcourt

on roadway design, 13

selecting solutions based on, 100–101

for umbrella, 83, 86

constructive criticism, 104, 108

containers, 100, 102, 118

cost-benefit analysis, 117

crash testing, 42

criteria, 52, 84

best solution fitting, 97, 98

for bike design, 10

for car design, 8

change in, 88, 90, 95

for container design, 118

for designs, 12, 51–53

identifying, 77

for lighting city streets, 84

for lunch line design, 21

for muffin design, 116

for raincoat design, 119

redefining, 86

for roadway design, 13

selecting solutions based on, 100–101

for umbrella, 83, 86

critical analysis, 108

cultural norms, 12

D

data

analysis and interpretation of, 61, 117

evaluating test data, 104

optimizing solutions with, 120

reproducibility of, 103

scientists and engineers' use of, 62

data collection, 104

decision-making tools, 76, 100–101, 102

decision matrix, 100, 100–102, 106, 113, 117, 131, 136

designed world, 6

design problem, 19, 48–50, 52, 54, 56–58, 65, 80–82

design process

analyze data, 136

ask questions, 22, 60, 81

background research, 99

beginning with a problem, 80

brainstorm solutions, 98–99, 113

collaborate, 22

combine the best parts of solutions, 154

communicate, 74, 136

conduct research, 74, 99, 136

consider constraints and criteria, 51–52, 84

consider trade-offs, 55

construct explanations and design solutions, 62

define problems precisely, 8, 21, 50–53, 60, 67, 73, 81, 82–86, 95, 135

develop and test solutions, 22, 50–64, 51, *51*, 54–55, 96–110

development of technology, 75

engage in argument from evidence, 62

establish criteria, 51–53, 84

evaluate advantages and disadvantages, 117

evaluate and test solutions, 102–108, 113, 129

evaluate data, 74, 104

examine needs to be met, 21, 52

identify and recommend a solution, 74, 136

identify the problem, 8, 21, 80–82

improving a promising solution, 116–119

make trade-off, 117

obtain, evaluate, and communicate information, 62

open-mindedness and, 99

optimize solutions, 51, 55, 114–126

redefine criteria and constraints, 86

reframing the problem, 88

research to define engineering problems, 87–90

review data and design, 104

select solution with decision-making tools, 100–101

test prototypes, 8, 117

diagram

cell phone communication network, 33

climate system, 39

design process, 103, 121

problems of open kitchen fires, 81

respiratory system, 29

tensile test, 60

difference between engineering and science practices, 59–62

Discuss, 6, 37, 50, 80, 98

Do the Math, 15, 41, 90, 92

Calculate the Amount of Material Needed, 54

Evaluating Parachute Designs, 105

Explain Change by Examining Interactions, 35

Stress-Strain Graph, 61

Use Math for Design Improvement, 118

Draw, 82, 106

drive train, *36,* 36–37

E

Earth system, 43–44

ecosystem, 28, *34,* 98

Edison, Thomas, 96, *109,* 109

effect

assessment of, 16, 17, 106

cause and, 36, 107

of a solution, 101

study of, 8, 14, 64, 66

of system interactions, 37

electrical engineer, 125–126

electrical system, *36,* 36–37

electric circuits in computers, 11

elk population, 34–35

energy

flow into and out of systems, 28

wind as source of, 109–110

engineered system

defined, 28, 30

interactions of, 33, 36–37

lock and dam system, 30

models and simulation of, 40

optimizing solutions, 120

video game system, 28

engineering, 6

careers in, 63–64, 125

cell phone communication network, 33

T

tables
- of advantages and disadvantages of engineered models, 41
- of criteria or constraints, 57, 58, 86, 94
- data for parachute design, 108
- of data for rocket design, 128
- of design options, 106
- of precisely stated problems, 82
- of questions, 2, 9
- Why It Matters, 2, 76

Take It Further
- Building on Earlier Solutions, 109–110
- Careers in Engineering: Civil Engineering, 63–64
- Designing an Efficient Lunch Line, 21–22
- Develop Solutions by Asking Questions, 22
- Modeling Earth Systems, 43–44
- People in Engineering: Ellen Ochoa, 125–126
- Redefining a Design Problems, 90–92

technical drawing, 112
technical illustration, 130
technology, 6
- aid to science, 7
- bike design, 10
- canned food, 9
- car design, 8
- computer development, 11
- development of, 75
- impact on environment, 14–16
- impact on society, 17–20
- influences on, 10–13, 25
- problem solving with, 1
- relationship to science and engineering, 6–9
- revision of, 16
- scientific tools, 6–7
- unintended impacts, 16, 25
- use of science and engineering, 59
telescope, 6

television, 12, *12*
tensile strength testing, *60*, 60–61
test data, 104, 123
test data analysis, 117
tool, 1, 6, 7, 12, 14, 19, 36, 40, 50, 51, 52, 53, 80, 94, 100, 101, 117, 120
tool, problem solving with, 1
trade-off, 55, 84, 101, 117, 124
transportation, 13, 18. *See also* **car.**
transportation system, 13
trebuchets, *78, 78*
treehouse design, *79, 79,* 88, *93,* 93–94, *94*
trend
- computer models illustrating, 39
- predicting, 38

U

umbrella design, 83
Unit Performance Task
- What is the best feature for a new pool entry ramp?, 135–136
- What is the best waste purification design?, 73–74
Unit Project
- Off to the Races, 77
- Solution Power!, 3
Unit Review, 69–72, 131–134
Unit Starter
- Asking Questions and Defining Problems, 3
- Identifying Criteria and Constraints, 77
unvented gas space heaters, 12
U.S. Clean Air Act, 11
U.S. Clean Water Act, 11

V

variables, 39, 60, 68, 105, 106–107, 123

W

water purification design, 73
water quality assessment, 98

water supply infrastructure, 17, *17*
weather forecasting, 27, 35, 39, 42, 45, 60
wheat, 15, 20, *20*
Why It Matters, 2, 76
wind, 91–92
Wind Tree, 90–92, *92*
wind turbines, 91–92
wolves, 34–35
wood, 10, 14, 15, 49, *49,* 65, *65,* 81, 88, 94, *94*
World Health Organization, 68
Wright Brothers, 130, *130*
Write, 11, 58

X

x-ray machines, 101

Y–Z

Yellowstone National Park, 34
yield point, 61–62